The Sentient Enterprise

The Sentient Enterprise

The Evolution of Business
Decision Making

Oliver Ratzesberger
Mohan Sawhney

WILEY

Published by John Wiley & Sons, Inc., Hoboken, New Jersey.
Published simultaneously in Canada.

For general information on our other products and services or for technical
support, please contact our Customer Care Department within the United
States at (800) 762–2974, outside the United States at (317) 572-3993, or fax
(317) 572-4002.

Wiley publishes in a variety of print and electronic formats and by print-on-
demand. Some material included with standard print versions of this book
may not be included in e-books or in print-on-demand. If this book refers to
media such as a CD or DVD that is not included in the version you purchased,
you may download this material at http://booksupport.wiley.com. For more
information about Wiley products, visit www.wiley.com.

Library of Congress Cataloging-in-Publication Data:

ISBN 978-1-119-43886-1 (Hardcover)
ISBN 978-1-119-43889-2 (ePDF)
ISBN 978-1-119-43879-3 (ePub)

Printed in the United States of America.

10 9 8 7 6 5 4 3 2 1

Contents

Foreword to *The Sentient Enterprise*

The Sentient Enterprise is both a good book and a good sign. Let me explain each component of that proclamation further.

It's a good book because two very smart and experienced gentlemen collaborated to produce some excellent advice on data and analytics. I've known both authors for over a decade, and they are, individually and collectively, powerful thought leaders.

Individually, either of these fellows could write an excellent book (and Sawhney has already written several!). Oliver Ratzesberger is one of the most visionary thinkers today on IT architecture issues. I was dazzled by the data architecture he created at eBay, and he's risen quickly to be the head of product at Teradata. That affiliation doesn't mean that he only espouses Teradata solutions; he's long been a strong advocate of open architectures and open-source tools like Hadoop.

Sawhney, trained as a marketing professor, is clearly much more than that. He's been a leading thinker for many years in the areas of innovation, digitization and e-business, networked organizations, and many other topics. If you were looking for a coauthor to think strategically about technology, you couldn't find anyone better than Mohan.

Collectively, the authors' expertise yields a unique set of topics that appeal to both strategists and practitioners—each of whom have an important stake in the journey toward sentience. One moment you're reading about how the massive explosion of data will reshape business and society. The next thing you know, you're learning how to prevent uncontrolled proliferation of virtual data marts with time-limited lifespans, or the correlation between call duration and customer sentiment in call centers. No one could accuse these authors of dwelling solely in either the strategic or the tactical realm.

The Sentient Enterprise is also a good sign that analytics are becoming a mainstream, professionally-managed activity—at least if organizations practice the lessons in this book. Historically, the creation of analytics was a somewhat unstructured and "artisanal" activity, driven by individual human hypotheses and curiosity. The analytical outcomes might be implemented by a decision maker, or they might not. There was no vehicle for embedding them into business processes and systems, or for learning from them across the organization.

But with the five "platforms" described in this book, analytics can move well beyond the artisanal stage. They are a linked set of capabilities for making analytics operational, production-based, and shared across the enterprise—a high-volume manufacturing operation for data and analytics-based decisions. They suggest a future—and a present in a few companies—in which analytical decisions are produced automatically and embedded into decisions and actions without much human intervention. For anyone who believes as I do that analytical decisions tend to be more accurate and less biased than those based on "the gut," this is great news.

These approaches won't be adopted for all decisions, at least not for a while. They currently apply to repetitive and tactical decisions based on a lot of data—much of it Internet-based "behavioral data," as Ratzesberger and Sawhney refer to it. In advertising, for example, versions of the platforms are already being used to support digital marketing decisions. But they won't be applied to decisions about Super Bowl ads anytime soon.

It's also important to remember, as the authors point out, that these platforms aren't just based on technology. Platforms consist of both technical and human capabilities. If you want the technical capabilities to succeed, you need a set of human skills, behaviors and attitudes that will make them possible. These human factors come into play both at the executive level—supporting development of the technical capabilities and their fit with business processes—and at the front lines as well.

In health care, for example, we desperately need approaches to "precision medicine," and they will require all of the five platforms that these authors describe. But part of those platforms are senior managers who are willing to sponsor the development of the platforms, and doctors and nurses who are willing to use them and work with their recommendations and decisions on a daily basis. It's anybody's guess whether developing the technological or the human capabilities will be more difficult, but both will be hard.

So get busy and start building these five platforms if you haven't done so already. Absorb both the strategic and tactical advice in this excellent book. And start preparing the wetware in your organization for a future in which analytical decisions are produced like high-quality widgets.

Thomas H. Davenport
Distinguished Professor, Babson College
Fellow, MIT Initiative on the Digital Economy
Author of *Competing on Analytics* and *Only Humans Need Apply*

Introduction

This is a book about business technology and business culture. Specifically, it's about how the right combination of technology and culture can transform the use of data and analytics so that even the largest organizations achieve new found levels of agility, insight, and value from their information sources.

This book is also written for a very wide range of business professionals. By that we mean not just senior technology executives and data scientists, but also business users, anyone who might have "analyst" in the job title, and pretty much everyone whose role is impacted by how data is gathered, analyzed and applied in the organization.

Whether you're establishing the next-generation digital strategy, setting up data experiments to explore deep neural networks, or establishing controls for access to your corporate KPI dashboard, this book is for you. Our goal is to build bridges across job functions and departmental silos to solve common challenges that most business professionals will recognize—challenges such as:

> *"How can we stop multiple teams from pulling information into their own data silos and then spending all our meeting time wondering why everyone's data doesn't match up?"*
>
> —Data scientist at a major auto manufacturer

> *"Just because we're big doesn't automatically mean we're the best; what's the best way to leverage our economy of scale while remaining agile?"*
>
> —Chief data officer for a telecommunications giant

> *"Why is it that my kids at home have self-service apps on their phones to build their own games, but I have to go through IT and a long requirements process every time I want to experiment with data?"*
>
> —Product testing analyst at an electronics manufacturer

"Given that our clients rely on us to be there tomorrow with the innovations they need, how can we get on a more predictive curve so any success we have today isn't just on borrowed time?"

—Senior VP for a profitable global networking company

These are tough questions from the many business perspectives you'll find across any company that relies on data (and in today's information-driven economy, which means pretty much *any company at all!*). Furthermore, these questions are not hypotheticals. They happen to be actual challenges relayed to us by top executives—from Dell, Verizon, General Motors, Siemens, Wells Fargo, and nearly a dozen other organizations we interviewed for this book—about the challenges they and their colleagues face on a daily basis.

Fortunately, these companies came up with innovative and scalable analytic solutions to address these challenges. In the pages to come, we'll examine these success stories and combine them with our own research and emerging best practices in big data and advanced analytics. In doing so, we'll chart a journey through what amounts to a new model for analytic capability, maturity, and agility at scale—something we call the Sentient Enterprise.

At its core, the Sentient Enterprise will change the way everyone in business makes decisions—from small, tactical decisions to mission-critical strategic decisions. We'll chart the path that technology and all of us who leverage it are taking to become more productive. The journey is as complex as it is valuable, so we've organized the Sentient Enterprise into a capability maturity model with five distinct stages:

1. The **Agile Data Platform** as the technology backbone for analytics capabilities and processes. Here is where outmoded data warehouse (DW) structures and methodologies are shifted to a balanced and decentralized framework, incorporating new technologies like cloud and are built for agility. Virtual data marts, sandboxes, data labs, and related tools are used in this stage to create the foundational technology platform for agility moving forward.

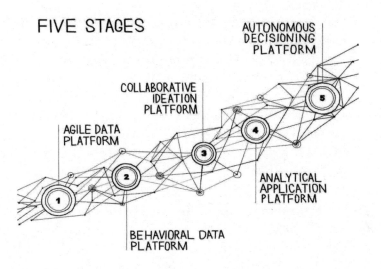

FIVE STAGES

AUTONOMOUS
DECISIONING
PLATFORM

COLLABORATIVE
IDEATION
PLATFORM

AGILE DATA
PLATFORM

ANALYTICAL
APPLICATION
PLATFORM

BEHAVIORAL DATA
PLATFORM

2. A **Behavioral Data Platform** that captures insights not just from transactions, but also from mapping complex interactions around the behavior of people, networks, and devices. Here is where enhanced job functions for the data scientist start to emerge. We also loop in CXOs and orient them to think in terms of behaviors and ultimately a customer-centric model. As we build this platform, Net Promoter Scores and other measures of customer sentiment and behavior get elevated to mission-critical importance for the enterprise.

3. The **Collaborative Ideation Platform** to let enterprises keep pace with the data explosion by socializing insights across the community of analytics professionals. With this platform, democratized data, crowdsourced collaboration, incentive-based gamification, and social connections within the enterprise can be leveraged together to connect humans and data in a fast, self-service manner that outperforms traditional centralized metadata approaches. As part of this platform, we build a "LinkedIn for Analytics" environment to analyze how people both use and talk about data in the organization. This includes social media conventions to see which ideas, projects, and people get followed, liked, shared, and tagged.

4. The **Analytical Application Platform** to leverage the simplicity of an exploding app economy for deployment of analytical capabilities across the broader business user community and to boost enterprise listening. In the process, we move away from static applications and extracting, transforming, and loading (ETL) in favor of self-service apps and self-awareness through enterprise listening. Visualizations now become more than just a pretty picture on an executive's wall; we instead put these visualizations to work to drive change and act on insights.

5. The **Autonomous Decisioning Platform**, where true sentience is achieved as the enterprise starts to act as an organism to make more and more tactical decisions on its own—without human intervention—so people can put more focus on strategic planning and major decisions. In this platform, we go beyond predictive technologies and increasingly deploy algorithms, machine learning, and even artificial intelligence (AI) at scale. This enables examination of all data to detect trends, patterns, and outliers as real-time context for human analysts and decision makers about shifts in behaviors. We take the bulk of data sifting and decisioning off people's shoulders and save human intervention for critical junctures. This is where true sentience is achieved in the enterprise.

While Chapters 3 through 7 deals sequentially with each of these five stages, it's important to remember that the journey is an ongoing one, and there is no single point of entry or completion. Think of the Sentient Enterprise as less a finish line than a North Star to guide your quest toward the strongest possible agility and value around data. The good news is that you don't have to do it all—and you don't have to do it all at once—in order to find plenty of big wins along the way.

ANALYTIC AWAKENING AT THE SCALE OF BUSINESS

Data is driving progress across all kinds of industries, but too many people—from analysts and business users to top C-suite decision makers—still don't know enough about how to innovate with it.

A few decades ago, this was enough rationale for most information technology (IT) leaders to dole out resources to the rest of their company colleagues through a stately and slow requirements-driven process. Sometimes that approach is still necessary. But in a world where every home, pocket, and purse has countless real-time and self-service apps, many companies are embarrassingly behind the curve in making data and analytic muscle more accessible to the diverse workforce that needs these resources to innovate.

On an organizational level, failing to leverage data for innovation and decision support can put your whole business on a downward trajectory. Success today requires navigating a constantly expanding data universe, and companies that don't fully embrace the data available to them are operating on borrowed time.

We'll explore in this book how the five-stage Sentient Enterprise capability maturity model can put data in the hands of more business users, part of a broader revolution into how companies listen to data, conduct analysis, and make autonomous decisions at massive scale in real time. In the process, we'll visit with top analytics professionals at some of today's largest and most successful organizations—Verizon, Dell, Cisco, General Motors (GM), Wells Fargo, and Siemens, just to name a few—to see how this revolution has, in many ways, already begun.

"We remind ourselves every day—it's even in our Company Credo—that being big is not the same as being the best," said Grace Hwang, Executive Director for Business Intelligence and Advanced Analytics at Verizon Wireless, one of the top executives who gave extensive interviews for the writing of this book. "Our job is to leverage economy of scale—but at the same time to be nimble and proactive."

In the pages to come, we've packed lots of real-world perspective from Verizon and other influential companies that have agreed to share their stories—their headaches and challenges, their insights and solutions—as they innovate their way to success. Throughout this book, in fact, we prioritize on-the-ground relevance and accessibility for a wide range of readers.

We've designed this book to be accessible and succinct for the lay business audience, with plenty of bread crumbs for more technophile information. While we are indeed talking about capabilities made possible by servers, nodes, data warehouses, and the skein of other infrastructure and software resources that go into any large analytics infrastructure, we do so from a perspective that's not too wonky or overly technical.

COLLABORATION WITHOUT CHAOS

Especially when working with many experts and massive infrastructure that might scale all the way to the global production level, it's easy for collaboration to veer into chaos if you don't have the proper platforms and hassle-free governance to help people stay in their lanes. But it's important for people to still collaborate effectively with those in other parts of the business, so silos don't develop as barriers to agility.

We'll see in the chapters to come how that one word—*agility*—is key to getting the enterprise to the sentient point where it can analyze data and make autonomous decisions at massive scale in real time. Agile systems and processes enable this by loosening IT roadblocks, democratizing data access, breaking down silos, and avoiding costly inefficiencies like data duplication, error, and just plain chaos.

Merriam-Webster's Collegiate Dictionary defines agile as "marked by ready ability to move with quick easy grace" or "having a quick resourceful and adaptable character." In the corporate world, business agility is usually defined as a company's ability to rapidly respond and adjust to change or adapt to meet customer demands. For our purposes, however, let's entertain a more targeted definition:

> Agility is the ability to decompose or break big problems
> and systems into smaller ones, so they're easier to solve
> and collaborate around.

In our effort to build this new agile environment for analytics, we looked across many industries for other examples of agility. This cross-industry perspective can solve problems in one sector by looking to other kinds of business settings for challenges met and lessons learned. The context may be different, but the insights and solutions can be strikingly similar.

For instance, we can learn much about an agile decomposition approach to tomorrow's data architectures by examining the Open Systems Interconnection (OSI) model that the telecommunications industry deployed as far back as the 1970s. OSI was developed to segment complicated infrastructure (wiring, relay circuits, software, etc.) into manageable chunks for better collaboration among various specialists.

By designing modular but interoperable parts of the system known as *abstraction layers*, OSI ensured that the work of software programmers, for instance, didn't conflict with what engineers and line workers might be doing in the field—or vice versa. We like the OSI example because, even though it was developed four decades ago, the technique of segmenting big systems into overlapping but distinct and manageable elements is a powerful ingredient for agility—one that we continue to see in some cutting-edge settings today.

Check out a technology called Docker (https://www.docker.com/) to see what we mean. Docker lets you break down the app-building process into a series of manageable steps. Through a simple Docker Engine and cloud-based Docker Hub, the company lets you assemble apps from modular components in a way that can reduce delays and friction between development, quality assurance (QA), and production environments. By breaking things down into smaller components, Docker aims to make the app-building process more manageable and reliable.

Another example is the entire "microservices" approach to building software architectures. Unlike traditional service-oriented architectures (SOAs) that integrate various business applications together, microservices architectures involve complex applications built from small, independent processes. These processes communicate with each other freely using application programming interfaces (APIs) that are language agnostic.

With microservices, you're still building powerful architectures; but it happens more efficiently, with modular elements broken down to focus on discrete small tasks. As a result, microservices architectures can be tremendously agile. They facilitate continuous-delivery software development and let you easily update or improve services organized around distinct capabilities such as user interfacing, logistics, billing, and other tasks.

AN EVOLUTIONARY JOURNEY (THAT'S ALREADY BEGUN!)

These examples show how we're on a journey away from monolithic and nonagile IT applications. But a caveat along this journey—one we'll emphasize often in the course of this book—is that you must fold in the *right kind of governance,* so your newly agile systems don't create more problems than they're solving. We'll talk through the Wild West pitfalls of data anarchy and error that arise when we try to loosen old systems and rules without putting some kind of (seamless and hassle-free) governance in place to support our new and agile methodologies.

We'll also see how most of the steps a company takes on the journey to sentience follow this definition of agility as decomposing problems into manageable components. The word is even embedded in the first of the Sentient Enterprise's five stages—the Agile Data Platform—proof of how front and center agility needs to be for anyone looking to survive and compete in today's data-driven marketplace.

Fortunately, we're not at square one in fulfilling the mandate for more agility and sentience around data in the enterprise; far from it! During his time at eBay, and now at Teradata, the practitioner on your coauthor team (Oliver) has worked to create collaborative and agile platforms for analytics. In the same spirit as OSI's abstraction layers, analytic platforms help data scientists and other users convene and extract insights around data safely and profitably.

The Sentient Enterprise now elevates this platform approach for collaboration to an entirely new and coordinated level at scale. Among other things, you'll learn about the Layered Data Architecture, which we'll discuss more fully in Chapter 2. In a nutshell, it's like an OSI-style nerve center for your data architecture—a tiered system for concurrent and customized access by many users of different skill levels and job descriptions.

Just as a telephone line worker is dispatched to run cable in the field while a systems traffic engineer is focused productively on routing options—without messing up the lines or each other's jobs—so the Layered Data Architecture keeps the operations analyst busy and supplied with data on key performance indicators (KPIs) without messing with source systems or fine-granularity modeling that the deep-dive data scientist is preoccupied with.

The Layered Data Architecture is, in turn, a foundation for the five complementary platforms that make up the Sentient Enterprise:

1. Agile Data Platform
2. Behavioral Data Platform
3. Collaborative Ideation Platform
4. Analytical Application Platform
5. Autonomous Decisioning Platform

By setting up an environment of five agile and closely linked platforms, we mature an organization's capabilities around data. That's why we refer to the Sentient Enterprise as a *"capability* maturity model"—not unlike the famous Six Sigma methodology for business processes and quality control—that many organizations can use as a yardstick for building capabilities and success.

A FRAMEWORK FOR AGILITY

As we'll discuss in Chapter 1, the Sentient Enterprise is the result of two very distinct but complementary perspectives on big data and analytics. For one of us (Mohan), the understanding of data's pivotal role in business has grown through many years as an academic researcher and corporate adviser. For the other (Oliver), the perspective comes from a long career as a technology executive and practitioner trying to manage the rewarding, often challenging, relationship a company keeps with its data and technology over time.

The two of us first compared notes in November 2013, and we have been iterating our way through this maturity model ever since. Our initial "aha" moment over a dinner meeting near Chicago was made all the more enticing by how fully our perspectives seemed to dovetail despite two very different careers. We aligned on how the right combination of technology, governance, and human engagement can launch enterprise analytics to new heights while preserving the coveted start-up-style agility that tends to atrophy at scale.

What was missing, however, was a framework for understanding and optimizing this alchemy so it can be replicated by any company with the vision and resources to try. After several years of joint collaboration and research, that framework now exists as the Sentient Enterprise, and this book is its manifesto.

Consider the Sentient Enterprise your road map for harmonizing analytic power, business practices, and human dynamics in ways that have already begun to transform and supercharge what's possible for big data and the industries that leverage it well. Inspired by our own progressive understanding of these trends over our careers and by the collaborative alchemy that has brought that evolution to the point we're at now, we're able to present the Sentient Enterprise to you as a viable framework for analytic agility, ready for application to your own business.

CHAPTER 1

Reimagining the Enterprise

The Stained Glass Bistro in Evanston, Illinois, is a bustling wine bar with impressive wine flights and a one-of-a-kind cheese and charcuterie plate. Nonetheless, your coauthors weren't paying much attention to the ambience during our dinner there together on November 12, 2013. By then, we were immersed in an animated conversation—begun hours before in Mohan's office, just a short walk away at the Kellogg School of Management—about the startling evolution now underway for analytics in large enterprises.

Introduced by our mutual friend Mary Gros, we had come together as two veteran technology professionals with decades of experience under our collective belts, trying to chart our industry from two very different perspectives: Mohan as an academic researcher, consultant, and technology company board member; Oliver as a longtime analytics practitioner and executive at major companies like eBay, Sears, and now Teradata Corporation.

As the ideas and the wine continued to flow around the table, we came to realize how our different perspectives were like complementary puzzle pieces that when fit together suddenly painted a clear picture of the journey that a data-driven enterprise needs to undertake. We began to see that rapid developments in technology and the explosion of data are now transforming the very nature of large enterprises—and that maturing analytics capabilities are the key to future survival.

Our insights that cold Tuesday in November were as enduring as they were sudden. Even the calendar date, 11/12/13, seemed auspicious as we began our own step-by-step journey in developing a capability maturity model for large data-driven companies, and putting it together in the book you're now reading. As you will see in the pages that follow, we're on an evolution toward an end state—a journey every big company should take, but only a few brave ones have started—that we call the "Sentient Enterprise."

We've since filled in the details of the five stages—the Agile Data Platform, the Behavioral Data Platform, the Collaborative Ideation Platform, the Analytical Application Platform, and the Autonomous Decisioning Platform—but everything is based on the insights sparked during that first meeting at the Stained Glass Bistro. Even the initial "Sentient Enterprise" term that we came up with over our dinner has endured: As we talked through the need to make decisions in real time and at the speed of data, with the enterprise ingesting information and using algorithms to make the bulk of decisions on its own, Mohan observed how such an enterprise was almost like an organism, a sentient organism . . . a "Sentient Enterprise."

The name stuck because it is persuasive not just as the title of a maturity model or a book, but because it summarizes the end state our whole analytics journey is leading us toward: the Sentient Enterprise is the North Star that every large business should aspire to as it struggles to make decisions at the speed of data.

DISRUPTION AND DECISION MAKING

Henry Ford is famous for reportedly (though not definitively) having said, "If I had asked people what they wanted, they would have said faster horses." By choosing instead to create the Model T automobile in 1908 and introduce the assembly line approach to production, he disrupted and redefined an entire mode of transportation. A century later, Steve Jobs fostered much the same attitude and outcome in developing the Apple iPhone, an instant and total game changer in how we view phones and mobile capabilities overall.

These are prime examples of disruptive innovation, a term coined only in 1995 but already a fixture in modern business theory and practice. Today, disregarding or deconstructing the status quo is embraced in countless business plans. Entrepreneurs are mounting wholesale reworkings of entire industries and product lines. Many investors put their money on the disruptive playbook, favoring the revolutionary over the incremental.

Serial disrupter Elon Musk is legendary for upending e-commerce with the 1998 advent of PayPal. Five years later, he echoed Henry Ford's makeover of the auto industry by founding Tesla Motors. From design and manufacturing to service and operation, Tesla's electric, software-intensive vehicles have redefined what the automobile can be today. (Full disclosure: both of us are proud Tesla owners and big fans of the company and its approach.) In a further instance of disruption, Tesla even released all of its patent holdings in 2014 in the belief that open-source innovation can accomplish more than any single company can achieve with its own proprietary ideas.

By definition, disruptive innovation displaces companies and sectors that remain vested in the status quo. There will always be losers. Borders Books and RadioShack, for example, are two retailers that failed to straddle the online/brick-and-mortar divide with seamless, multichannel customer engagement models. They learned the hard way how disruption and bankruptcy share the same linguistic root.

Modern analytics, however, raises the stakes and brings disruption to another scale altogether. As data-driven becomes the norm across all industries, we're no longer just facing obsolescence of particular products, sectors, or services; we're now seeing the extinction of fundamental business models that most major companies have been founded on.

Indeed, big data and the new analytic capabilities that go along with it are changing everything from how large enterprises structure and finance operations to how they pursue opportunities and engage their workforce. And analytics can revolutionize an organization's ability to listen to data sources, understand what the data is saying, and use it to make informed decisions in near real time.

SELF-DISRUPTION AT CISCO: ON PURPOSE AND AT SCALE

Foundational writings on disruption are required reading for anyone in business today. So embedded is the concept, in fact, that the question is no longer how and why disruption happens, but who the winners and losers are. That has given rise to a second wave of insight around the mantra to "disrupt or be disrupted" (a very large wave indeed, judging by the 14 million search results when we recently Googled the term).

Consider the case of Cisco Systems, a hugely successful global networking company that includes more than 70,000 employees and 240,000 industry partners. Some 80 percent of the world's networking traffic crosses Cisco infrastructure at some point in time; the company consistently ranks number one or two in every market where it competes. Still, Cisco is pursuing an aggressive and company-wide self-disruption effort as if its survival depends on it. That's because it does!

We recently caught up with Kevin Bandy, senior vice president and chief digital officer for Cisco Systems. As he shared Cisco's self-imposed transformation from a hardware-intensive model to a software- and consumption-based model focused on recurring revenue, Kevin explained that the company is not racing so much against competitors, but against the future needs of its own customers.

"Business models are changing every 18 to 24 months with Moore's law," he told us. "Our trigger to change was the voice of our customers and the forward visibility they expect us to have when it comes to innovation and how they'll be consuming it in the future."

Marathon runners know to hydrate before they get thirsty. The same can be said of companies needing to self-disrupt before they get desperate. "Rather than let someone else disrupt us, we chose to disrupt ourselves," Kevin explained. "That's especially critical with the operational level we're at; 80 percent of global networking traffic is too important to let fail."

SELF-DISRUPT IN SUSTAINABLE WAYS

When you're a small start-up, disruption is like intellectual Red Bull that powers you through a few market cycles. You're agile because you're small. And you can risk a huge crash because, given how 90 percent of start-ups fail within a few years, long-term survival is mostly an abstraction.

Large enterprises, with an ecosystem of customers relying on them, can't afford to think this way—but neither can they afford to sit still. To thread the needle, big companies like Cisco are fostering disruption and entrepreneurialism within the context of sustainable and scalable models. You're building a digital operating model of people, processes, behaviors, and competencies in the spirit of what the Wharton School's Eric Clemons calls an "all-pervasive" approach to disruption across the "structure and strategy of the entire business."

Unless you're constantly anticipating tomorrow, even today's biggest successes will always be on borrowed time. This is especially true in analytics, where clients may be buying not just a product but an entire digital environment that their whole business relies on.

"Think about the logic of Moore's law, and the reality that corporate timetables for standing up innovation at scale can be 18 to 24 months," explained Kevin. "If it's only then that we realize we stood up the wrong solution, we can spend another two years of unraveling and rebuilding. That whole cycle counts for eons on the technology clock—plenty of time to put yourself and your customers out of business if you make the wrong call."

Cisco's story shows how, especially for large enterprises that serve in a trusted adviser role, getting ahead of disruption is a make-or-break proposition. Whatever customers think of you now, they'll abandon you—or go out of business along with you—if you're not there with the right innovations needed for tomorrow.

"The further along you go on this Sentient Enterprise maturity model, you encounter the challenge of people relying on you," echoes Brett Vermette, director of big data infrastructure and platform engineering at General Motors. "Delight becomes demand. Experiment becomes expectation."

We interviewed Brett about GM's own proactive transformation to consolidate what turned out to be hundreds of disconnected data marts into a more unified and agile environment. "We had an intensive, six-week period in early 2013, launching our enterprise data warehouse program," he told us. "This was a major transformation program, including installation of 60 crates of infrastructure in our data center, building the foundation for a global data warehouse, and consolidation of more than 200 siloed repositories and data marts over time.

"As part of our IT transformation, GM hired thousands of new college graduates and experienced IT professionals to handle work previously done by third-party suppliers," Brett said. "We were fortunate to have top leadership support; the challenge was more how to mobilize company-wide in ways that remained agile and innovative. It's like fighting the agility war on all fronts." In Chapter 3, we'll take a closer look at how GM achieved success in this effort.

ANALYTIC PAIN POINTS AND A SELF-SERVICE REVOLUTION

GM is a manufacturing company with roots going back more than a century. The fact that such a legacy institution would embrace analytics shows just how fully data has penetrated all markets and industries. Indeed, financial implications for this global tsunami of digitized information are so important that the World Economic Forum has now designated big data as a new kind of economic asset, just like currency or gold.

A study by the MIT Center for Digital Business, meanwhile, is representative of many in showing how data-driven businesses do indeed have the edge. That survey of 330 leading U.S. businesses showed companies that focused strongly on data-driven decision making had an average of four percentage points higher productivity and six percentage points higher profits overall.

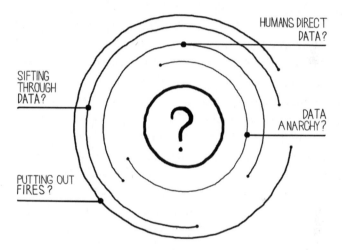

Many businesses nonetheless struggle through a combination of huge data volumes and organizational hurdles that creates analytic pain points familiar to any data scientist who works at scale. For one thing, we spend the majority of our time just sifting through data instead of making decisions. We're constantly on our heels in reaction mode, putting out fires instead of charting the future. We can't seem to make decisions fast enough, given that our brains don't scale the way data can.

Consensus among computational neuroscientists puts the human brain's storage capacity somewhere between 10 and 100 terabytes. Compare that to a worldwide data explosion that's more than a trillion gigabytes annually (1,000 gigabytes = 1 terabyte) and on track to hit 30 exabytes (or 30 billion gigabytes) every month by 2020—and you begin to see the root of nearly all our enterprise challenges and opportunities.

Success involves recognizing the changing nature of both data and the human expectations and interactions around that data as technology transforms the entire world into an on-demand, self-service community. A recent study by Forrester Research showed 73 percent of online customers consider time as their most important customer service priority, while another survey showed three-quarters of consumers prefer to solve customer service issues on their own.

Self-service has even come to dominate tasks involving personal or sensitive information, like accessing insurance records or checking in at a doctor's office. Among the other data points, a *Harvard Business Review* report found self-service on the rise in restaurants; and back in 2013, a large Cisco survey of consumers in 11 different countries found 61 percent were willing to shop in a completely automated store. Now the advent of Amazon Go has made that a viable and widespread option.

Self-service options have revolutionized the average person's ability not just to receive products and information, but to create them, too. A prime example is the do-it-yourself mobile app creation trend, with the advent of the software development kit (SDK) or devkit putting advanced software development skills at virtually anyone's fingertips.

In 2011, for example, a 14-year-old named Robert Nay used a free version of Corona SDK to create Bubble Ball, a mobile game for iPhone, iPad, and Android that was downloaded 400,000 times the first day of its release and went on to unseat Angry Birds from its No. 1 spot in the Apple Store. Robert programmed the game all by himself in just over a month's time. If this is how far we've come in the realm of shopping and games, you begin to see why nearly every employee working today within data-driven companies is clamoring for the same freedom around business intelligence and analytics.

ACCESS AND CONTROL

Imagine for a moment that you're a midlevel data scientist at a large corporation. Back home, your teenage kid can follow Robert Nay's example and use a free online devkit to manipulate everything from audio, graphics, cryptography, and networking to device information like accelerometer, GPS, and user input data.

Unfortunately, while he runs along to school to show off his new smash-hit game to classmates, you run to the office and smash your fist against your IT department's door, demanding why it is going to take 18 months to get that data research project done for your finance department to make decisions about asset allocation!

You're a resourceful employee, so when you don't get a good answer or a better time line, you find a better way. You quickly build a data mart—a collection of copies from the company's broader data infrastructure—that you customize for your own specific business needs: in this case, finance. In short order, this data mart is churning out insights that feel useful and relevant. This is your ticket to agility in a demanding environment where time to market is everything.

The problem is that data that may seem useful turns out to be unruly; information that seems relevant could be just plain wrong. It seems your own little slice of the company's data is copying information and introducing data drift—the unpredictable and unending mutations of data caused by operations, maintenance, updating, and replatforming of databases. You've just created chaos in the guise of agility. This is one of many nightmare scenarios that are anything but hypothetical; they're the unfortunate reality for most large enterprises today.

These problems of control, access, and value around data are nothing new. Before our first meeting in Evanston, we had each given dozens of keynotes and lectures on various parts of the picture. Oliver routinely shared with business leaders the trials, tribulations, and opportunities that came with his having built production-scale analytic capabilities from the ground up. Mohan, meanwhile, had been making similar rounds with executive audiences from his vantage point as a busy researcher, consultant, and board member of a public company with more than 1,500 analytics professionals.

Presentations tend to be one-way conversations, however. So it was a revelation for the two of us to finally meet, compare notes, and hit upon a vision for the future. We realized how Oliver had been in the trenches and Mohan had been in the clouds. Long before the term *big data* became popular, Oliver was toiling at ground zero, living through a larger analytic journey that he was too busy to recognize or name. Mohan, meanwhile, was looking at the same dynamics from 30,000 feet, charting broad industry trends without the "how to" insights that made up most of Oliver's daily life. At last, our combined perspectives connected the dots between things like vision, strategy, finance, and execution.

This expanded dashboard—our combined perspectives on our data-driven economy—brought new clarity to both the pitfalls and the payoffs involving huge growths in data volumes, complexity, and velocity. Today, well over 1.7 megabytes are generated per minute for every person on Earth. Much of this growth involves so-called behavioral data, which are all those events and data points in between or across transactions. These are the bread crumbs and fingerprints, derived from both human- and machine-generated data, which let us chart behavioral patterns and understand interactions. We no longer just count or aggregate data points; we are now connecting them in complex ways.

One of the side effects of dealing with behavioral data, however, is an explosion in data volumes that quickly outpaces our ability to extract insights. Whether you're talking about metadata management or related techniques to assign meaning and value, the simple fact is that our human brains don't scale the way data does. For every product manufactured there can be hundreds or thousands of data points leading up to the assembly. And for every purchase transaction there can be more than a hundred interactions, especially with e-commerce.

Think of the humble visit to a brick-and-mortar store in the era before big data, or even today. By our own estimates, that process of walking the aisles and buying something at checkout may create about 100 bytes of data involving the item, the price, credit card information, and probably not much more information than that.

By comparison, today's average visit to an online retail site can generate hundreds of kilobytes of data—everything from the items and customer reviews you viewed (and for how long) to what products you placed in your online shopping cart and whether they stayed there through checkout. Any one of these points is subject to analysis and further generation of data.

It has been said that what you can learn from an online customer today is akin to tracking every single step during a physical visit to a store; it's like having a GoPro video camera mounted on the head of every customer who walks through the door, and then collecting and analyzing the entire video stream, frame by frame. But if you don't have structures to capture and responsibly manage that data—including provisions for privacy, data protection, and information security that we'll talk about toward the end of this book—then you won't really be able to leverage that information as fully and responsibly as possible.

A NECESSARY EVOLUTION

These and other issues reverberated in our heads long after our first meeting in Evanston. Over the next days and weeks—in airplanes and taxis, in gaps between meetings and other spare moments—we formulated a nascent framework to align our thoughts and energy. We kept in touch throughout, and every call and e-mail helped flesh out our understanding of what has become the Sentient Enterprise journey.

The more we aligned, the more we were able to understand that this journey is an evolutionary one that is disrupting entire industries and changing the very nature—the very identity—of large companies across nearly all sectors of our economy. Many talk about what the enterprise can do with data and analytics; but it's crucially important to also understand just what data and analytics are doing to big business.

As Cisco's and GM's own stories earlier in this chapter make clear, no industry is safe from disruptions in how we leverage data and data products, and no large company can afford to sit on the fence. Big data is a disruptive and unstoppable wave, and the leaders who drive change in their organizations are the ones who recognize they have no choice but to become disrupters themselves, before some other company does it first.

These pressing realities position the Sentient Enterprise journey as a necessary evolution for survival—a mandate rather than an option. It's what we call "change management on steroids," and we need to heed the clarion call for change in ways that don't make the problem worse.

We'll explore in these pages, for instance, how important it is to democratize access to data throughout your organization for faster decision making. And we'll see how the key to scaling insights and keeping your business user community aligned is to tailor the environment for maximum collaboration—a "LinkedIn for Analytics" approach that borrows lessons from social media, gaming, and other areas where users naturally are driven to engage.

We can't achieve this agility, however, through shortcuts like throwing away documentation and governance. That kind of Wild West approach will do more harm than good via data drift, duplication, and destructive information anarchy. There are many such challenges in the overall bid to adapt our technology to the needs of our employees, customers, and the entire business ecosystem.

PUTTING IT ALL TOGETHER

A couple of months after first connecting in Evanston, the two of us met again, this time in San Diego, to flesh out more fully what this evolution toward the Sentient Enterprise looked like. We were certain by then that our collaboration around this journey was an important one that was just waiting to be rendered. In fact, our mutual friend and Oliver's Teradata colleague, Mary Gros, arranged for our discussion to be literally rendered by a graphic artist who joined us in a conference room overlooking the nearby peak of Mount Woodson. As the artist scribbled away, we talked through a skein of insights until we aligned on five foundational qualities that define the Sentient Enterprise.

The Sentient Enterprise is:

- **Proactive** and able to sense micro-trends signaling the next crisis or the next opportunity.
- **Frictionless** in that it can act as one organism, human and machine, without any impedance or bottlenecks created by silos.
- **Autonomous** in its ability to listen to data and make decisions in real time without too much human intervention.
- **Scalable** to virtually any size company, with the ability to leverage unlimited amounts of data for making decisions.
- **Evolving** through intelligence that is native and emergent.

In short order, we continued to refine this journey into its systematic, five-stage evolution and hit the road with a joint slide presentation to executives at the Walt Disney Company, Boeing, BMW, and other major corporations. As the nods of agreement added up in boardrooms and C-suites around the world, we knew we had to take the next step and write the book you're now reading.

As mentioned in the Introduction, our long-term vision for the Sentient Enterprise is not unlike the popular Six Sigma model for manufacturing in that we've established a specific framework for excellence that can be broadly applied. Just as Six Sigma has been modeled by countless business strategists since its inception by Motorola in 1986, our hope is that the five-stage Sentient Enterprise model will gather momentum across the many industries that rely on data for decision making and value.

Like Six Sigma, the Sentient Enterprise is a business phenomenon that is already underway, yet always aspirational. We can and will always do better. But we have seen enough of the Sentient Enterprise puzzle in place to know it's a viable model for orders-of-magnitude leaps in business performance and value that aren't really possible any other way. It's the threaded needle, the secret sauce, a recipe for agility and productivity at any scale.

CHAPTER 2

Leveraging an Expanding Universe of Data

Bay is a multibillion-dollar corporation with operations in more than 30 countries. Founded in 1995, the San Jose–based company is an early Internet pioneer that has managed to grow through changing markets and economic conditions to become the global e-commerce powerhouse it is today. Given such long-term resilience and success, it's easy to forget the considerable growing pains eBay suffered in the mid-2000s. That's when the company's core auction business began to plateau, putting eBay at a crossroads.

"Is eBay becoming a mature company that won't be able to keep up its heady growth?" asked a Wharton School report in February 2005, amid disappointing stock performance and a reduced financial outlook for that year. An October 2007 *Fortune* article, meanwhile, chronicled "eBay's transition to adulthood" as the company sought more growth through acquisitions and weathered a shift in how analysts valued the company—from web-centric statistics like new users and total auction listings to retail-industry metrics like overall sales growth and revenue generated per user.

These two citations are representative of many from the mid-2000s, and they fall within the tenure of the practitioner in your practitioner/academic coauthor team (Oliver), who served in senior analytics roles at eBay from November 2004 through October 2011. It was a time when analytics suddenly became a target for further growth and investment internally, as eBay realized the valuable role data and data products could play as a chief differentiator moving forward. eBay had begun collaborating on advertising with partners like Yahoo! and Google, for example, and those partners saw huge value in eBay's traffic and customer data. Analytics, in other words, became a top-line business driver almost overnight.

We'll share details later in this chapter on how some clutch moves by the eBay analytics team during this crucial period helped revitalize the company and laid groundwork for some core elements of the Sentient Enterprise approach. But first we need to recognize how these early efforts to prioritize analytics came in response to industry-wide changes that are still happening today.

A UNIVERSE OF DATA: EXPANDING EXPONENTIALLY WITH NEW SOURCES

Embracing analytics as a market differentiator is now a rite of passage for any business reaching maturity or hoping to stay competitive in today's thoroughly data-driven economy. And analytics will only get more valuable as we find more—and more diverse—forms of data to fuel our inquiries. Indeed, the exponential growth in data volumes, complexity, and velocity makes the consequences and payoffs from how we leverage analytics all the more steep.

Research from the marketing intelligence firm IDC shows our digital universe is expanding 40 percent per year and is expected to hit 44 zetabytes (one zetabyte is a trillion gigabytes) by 2020. That's more than all the stars in the universe. A recent Cisco Visual Networking Index, meanwhile, projects more than 10 billion mobile-ready devices and connections by 2018, with average mobile connection speeds doubling by then to 2.5 megabytes per second. These are some of the dynamics behind the fact that 1.7 megabytes are being generated per minute for every person on Earth. But that doesn't mean all that data is being generated by people.

It turns out that online shopping behavior and other forms of human-generated data—like when someone types on a keyboard, takes a picture, hits the "record" button, or scans a bar code—are dwarfed by the so-called Internet of Things (IoT), made up of data from electronic sensors and other machine-generated sources. These "things" can be environmental sensors monitoring weather, traffic, or energy grid patterns; telemetry from machines, trucks, or store shelves to track manufacturing and distribution channels; and wearable devices that relay data about your health, location, and activity level.

Those examples are just the tip of the iceberg. With the IoT figuring prominently among its Top 10 Strategic Technology Trends, Gartner forecast some 26 billion IoT units installed by 2020 and IoT product and service suppliers generating more than $300 billion in revenue and $1.9 trillion in global economic value. IDC's research, meanwhile,

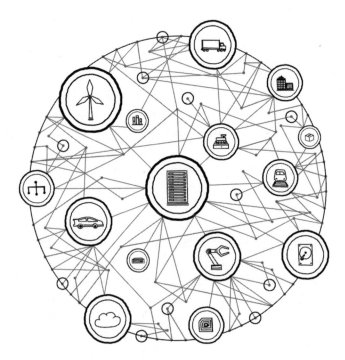

shows that sensor signals from embedded systems—a major IoT component—currently make up only 2 percent of the digital universe, but will reach 10 percent by the end of the decade.

The IoT continues to index our world on an unprecedented, granular level. As capacity grows, so do the chances to reap—or miss out on—immense value for your organization through analytics. The key to navigating our world's growing digital footprint lies in all the interactions and behaviors we see happening amid all that information.

In its simplest forms, analytics can achieve the straightforward goal of capturing transactions for a specific purpose. From there it can lead to: "Now that I've got those transactions, what else can I learn, and how else can I optimize?" With the IoT, you're suddenly dealing with a wider and more complex variety of data; and that means the possibilities grow exponentially as you figure out new ways to apply that data for analysis and learning.

Take the example of fleet logistics. The immediate value of a GPS sensor in a tractor trailer includes answers to questions like: "Where's my truck? Did my driver take too long a break or did he stop somewhere that's not on the scheduled route?" That immediate interest is very transactional. But look subsequently at your fleet GPS data in aggregate over time, and you are led to some very interesting use cases for saving time and fuel through efficient route processing and other logistics.

Sensors in wind turbines, meanwhile, record efficiency ratios and other metrics for immediate transactional needs like repair or warranty issues. But keeping track from an analytics perspective can also help you leverage that information as input for future decisions around design criteria or placement of new turbines.

The growing list of use cases includes everyday examples like the so-called black-box event data recorders in most new cars, with metrics around driving habits and vehicle performance that can serve transactional needs like fuel efficiency and crash investigations, as well as predictive needs like engine and safety design modifications in new models. And passenger cars are increasingly able to automatically capture and transmit diagnostics for future purposes like scheduling maintenance and repairs, as well as real-time needs.

For instance, one of us (Mohan) had trouble starting a Tesla in the driveway on a very cold February morning. Thanks to remote diagnostics systems that deliver real-time information, one call to the service center allowed a service representative to immediately log into the car and benchmark its power consumption against that of other Teslas within a 50-mile radius. Pinpointing the problem as cold starts, the technician advised preheating the battery for a few minutes, something easily done via app from inside the house. That's the future of service in an IoT world: zero-touch and real-time repairs!

Cars may one day be able to order their own replacement parts, or even connect with a consumer's 3D printer to create the part at home in the garage. Especially when we combine multiple existing technologies—black-box sensors and 3D printers in this case—get ready to see entire business models redefined in radical ways.

Of course, black boxes have been in airplanes a lot longer than they've been in cars; the devices (which are actually colored orange) have been mandatory in U.S. commercial jets since 1967. Today's sensor revolution, however, allows modern black boxes to assess airplane and crew behavior with unprecedented clarity. And now The Boeing

Company is leading an effort to increase connectivity among multiple black boxes! Boeing has filed patents for a system that would link the data from many black boxes, helping give aviation experts a granular and fleetwide understanding of how planes are operating and where problems may lie.

Not surprisingly, Siemens is another company that's pioneering connectivity, data integration, and analysis on an unprecedented scale. Founded in 1847, the global engineering powerhouse employs more than 340,000 people worldwide, with annual revenue upwards of $86 billion. The company recently implemented a common technology base that processes more than 17 terabytes of data per month for remote monitoring and maintenance of more than 300,000 connected devices—everything from traffic light controls and locomotives to computed tomography (CT) scanners and the sensor-laden wind turbines we mentioned a few paragraphs back.

Gerhard Kress is vice president of data services at Siemens Mobility, the division that focuses on railway vehicles and control systems. "The sensor data from just one fleet of trains in Europe can fill about 100 billion lines of a table," he told us. "The right analytics on all this data can let us know—a week or two in advance—that a component on a train is going to fail, and we can take steps to stop or minimize the problem before it happens. That's something we couldn't have done just a few years ago." (We'll have a closer examination of Siemens's groundbreaking success at predictive maintenance in Chapter 7.)

Whether the goal is improving reliability, boosting efficiency, or saving lives, it's pretty powerful and exciting to see how a combination of human-generated data and the IoT can help us detect learned behaviors and patterns from various data sources to guide proactive interventions and future decisions in very specific and accurate ways.

GAME-CHANGING CAPABILITIES

We've stressed how data is transforming countless industries for competitive advantage. Perhaps nowhere is this analytic quest for competitive advantage taken more literally than in our national pastime: baseball.

Perhaps you're familiar with *Moneyball*, the data-driven Cinderella story about how the 2002 Oakland Athletics used player statistics and algorithms to build a winning baseball team. From an analytics perspective, the closest your coauthors ever got to "inside baseball" on the subject came by way of a 2016 technology summit at a seaside conference center in Half Moon Bay, California. One session in particular, featuring Bill Schlough, senior vice president and chief information officer for the San Francisco Giants, made clear how far the sport has come since the early days of *Moneyball*.

For instance, when *Moneyball* innovator Billy Beane first put analytics in service for Oakland, he was focused mostly on scouting talent through the use of relatively small sets of historical data. Most of it was high-level summary data about players' past performance. Today, advanced radar can help make critical decisions in the middle of the game.

Sensors track not just the speed of a ball, but also the arc and spin to help determine if a pitcher is getting fatigued. "You can use this data to detect when the rotation on the ball is starting to slow—it's not breaking as much as it was before on previous pitches," said Bill Schlough. "That's a sign that your pitcher may be about to give up a run; and that's the kind of information the coach can use to pull him from the mound before that happens."

At the point we caught up with Bill in October 2016, the Giants were enjoying a 490-home-game sellout streak at the team's 41,000-seat stadium.

While Bill had to be careful not to discuss competitive advantage, our time together with him revealed enough for us to understand how one of the most successful franchises in baseball also happens to be heavily driven by analytics.

"Willie Mays was once asked about the pitcher he feared most, and his answer was, 'Show me a pitcher I've never seen.' That's why, when we host another team, our sensors track how their pitchers throw," Bill said. "So, what's to stop you from programming those dynamics into a pitching machine?"

The Giants also embrace technology to optimize engagement with entire demographic groups among its fan base. Take the case of millennials. "No millennial is going to sit still for a three-hour game with two hours and 40 minutes of dead time and 20 minutes of action," Bill said. "That's why we have full Wi-Fi connectivity and TVs in the lounge areas, so it's like a huge sports bar where they can follow multiple games."

WELL-INTENTIONED ANARCHY

For all its promise across diverse industries and applications, today's massive flood of information can reap top value only if you embrace architectures that support the kind of workplace collaboration we talked about in this book's Introduction. Otherwise, we're stuck in a reactive and very confusing situation. Consider a story that perhaps you can relate to:

> A couple of weeks before the Q4 earnings call, the CFO of a telecommunications company receives sales and revenue numbers for the quarter and notices a five percent dip in revenue. She calls her executive team together and assigns them the task of trying to figure out why. Her team is divided on whether the number is even accurate. Those analysts who agree with it suggest that this dip is just fallout from the problems that the company started having with service issues back in January when several snowstorms hit major East Coast and Midwest urban areas hard.

> The company was never able to fully recover from angry customers canceling their contracts, and analysts are not really sure why the company kept losing them, even in the sunny summer months. These problems, compounded by a decline in discretionary consumer spending and a competitor's new contract with the iPhone, are only now just becoming apparent. The analysts sigh and say this might just have to be the status quo everyone needs to accept.

Unfortunately, this scenario is all too common. It depicts a company that's reactive instead of proactive, and is far too sluggish in identifying small problems before they snowball into catastrophic ones.

It turns out that more than half (57 percent) of the 362 global executives in a recent survey by the Economist Intelligence Unit said that important business data is not captured or shared at their companies. Furthermore, 42 percent said that their data is cumbersome and not user-friendly.

True agility requires us to break down silos so that a variety of professionals from across the organization can work together around data to unlock new insights. At the same time, we need to be careful in how we break down those silos and what kind of governance we put in their place, or else we'll suffer through the analytics pain points mentioned in Chapter 1. Yes, we need to make data accessible. But we can't be very agile if doing so leaves our organization swamped in a mess of incoherent data—a good deal of it duplicated or wrong because we don't have the systems or governance to manage it well.

DATA MARTS AND THEIR DISCONTENTS

Remember our scenario in Chapter 1, where our midlevel data scientist didn't feel like waiting a year and a half for an official IT solution? He got resourceful and built his own data mart, a business-unit-specific silo that copies the data he needs so he can get his project done more quickly. Unfortunately, his rock-star solution is throwing rocks into the system. Here's why:

Data marts create data drift, which happens when data loading and maintenance aren't coordinated. This results in mismatched structures and redundancy that lead to inconsistent answers. Let's assume, for instance, that you have the CMO controlling one data mart and the CFO controlling another, and they're trying to pull the same metric—let's say the metric is the number of active customers this month. They'll likely come up with very different numbers because of misaligned databases, hardware, software platforms, and reporting tools that make it difficult or impossible to standardize and integrate information.

In our own experience, we've seen how data marts can lead to unnecessary duplication by a factor of 20 times or more, with data drift of 60 percent or more. The costs here are not abstract, and they go beyond the capacity and memory for all that unnecessary duplication. Imagine that the skewed data your CFO and CMO are working with involves promotional materials targeted to VIP customers. How much time, effort, and money are going toward sending marketing collateral and special offers to the wrong customers?

Given these costs, the redundant data operations, and hours of discussion about how to recalibrate misaligned metrics, we've gotten used to saying—only half-jokingly—that "data marts simply can't be cheap enough to justify their existence." Nothing about them is agile; it's the Wild West, and these data silos are Public Enemy Number One.

This is all a troubling picture not just because of the bad data and lost market opportunities that result, but also because of the effect it has on workforce culture and performance. Think about it: We hire people to be intelligent and proactive and to get things done. We pay recruiters top dollar to get folks who think outside the box and inno- vate through challenges. These are the qualities that drive success. Unfortunately, that gut feeling of success and agility the go-getters have when building a data mart is just a mirage; the reality is that the organization has actually become less agile because of data anarchy and ballooning IT costs to handle all the redundancies.

The road to data anarchy may be paved with good intentions, but it still leads us to the point where the majority of people's time can be spent on the fallout from this setup. Think of the daily or weekly fire drills that take place when numbers don't match up and the circular arguments begin over which data is right and which data is wrong. Users and technology executives alike can get stuck spinning their wheels if the organization doesn't have systems and policies that are inclusive and effective around data.

Business users sequestered from the analytic tools they need tend to either give up or go it alone through stovepipes and silos. It's no wonder that user frustration can arise under these circumstances. In *Drive*, his best-selling book on workplace motivation, author Daniel Pink explains how scientists have developed a "new operating system" for business success that revolves around three elements: autonomy, or the urge to direct our own lives; mastery, the desire to get better and better at something; and purpose, the yearning to do something that matters. It's not hard to look at these insights and see how most current IT policies and methodologies come up woefully short.

A SOLUTION? "LINKEDIN FOR ANALYTICS"

We talked in Chapter 1 about the rapidly changing expectations around data, with users from all walks of life now demanding real-time interaction. And they expect low latency; a Google study, in fact, showed it takes only 250 milliseconds for a user to get tired of waiting for a site to load. That's literally less than the blink of an eye! These factors are driving a new self-service ethic where everyone expects to be able to access data quickly and in ways that suit his or her own needs. Your own employees have these expectations as well.

Standing up the technological systems in the workplace to meet these internal expectations is tough, but business users don't care! When you tell members of your finance or marketing department it may take up to 18 months to complete an intensive data research project, don't be surprised when they set up their own data mart. They don't care that the supposed agility they perceive is actually polluting the larger analytics environment with data anarchy that leads to inconsistent or just plain wrong answers.

To keep business users aligned and engaged, we must tailor the analytics to them. For this, we borrow lessons from social media, gaming, and other areas where people naturally—even compulsively—want to take part.

It's important to preview a crowdsourcing approach, "LinkedIn for Analytics," we'll learn more about in Chapter 5. It's not related to the LinkedIn company, just inspired by that social media platform. The idea is to bring to analytics that same culture of engagement you see on LinkedIn and many other social platforms or gaming environments. And it solves some key concerns about scalability in the process.

If you have a fairly small operation, you may be able to survive with a traditional approach like having your centralized team of analysts assign metadata so the rest of the company knows what information is important and where to find it. But in large organizations dealing with big data today, that traditional approach can quickly break down. Humans don't scale the way data does, and a corps of a hundred or even a thousand analysts still won't be able to keep up with the job of documenting the huge volumes of information and lightning-fast data streams coming at them.

That's why we need to turn to the wisdom of the crowd; specifically, the hundreds or thousands of people within your organization who work with data. At its core, LinkedIn for Analytics is essentially analytics on your analytics community. It starts with algorithmic models to examine what your community of data scientists and other analysts is doing with data, but we're not simply interested in their specific queries or dashboard activity. We want to provide a forum to capture and analyze commentary and discussion between these folks, complete with social media conventions to let people "like" a certain analytic approach, "follow" a particular analyst, or monitor visualizations and data sets that are popular and trending.

Suddenly, these patterns you see in the kinds of ideas, projects, and people that get followed, shared, and liked help you answer questions such as: "Who are the influencers?" "What projects and ideas are gathering the most energy?" "What does this tell us about the most important projects and their potential success outside the organization?" These insights open up infinite possibilities for innovation within your company.

We're not the first to crowdsource technical innovation by leveraging inherent human tendencies. The U.S. Department of Defense sponsors an online "shredder challenge" contest, with a $50,000 prize for whoever can best reconstruct documents that have been mercilessly shredded, with the shards then posted online. In another case, medical researchers used a gaming approach to help map a crucial AIDS enzyme (think Tetris for a good cause).

The end result is a business user community aligned and engaged in the task of tailoring and safely experimenting with data around the business problems they care about most. And just like the rest of the social media world, the best solutions go viral.

GETTING BACK TO EBAY: FULFILLING THE ANALYTICS MANDATE

By now, you probably see how any practical and scalable implementation of next-generation analytics in the enterprise demands we strike a careful balance between agility, governance, and a culture of inclusion around data. In the next handful of chapters that deal with each of the five stages of the Sentient Enterprise capability maturity model, we'll show in detail how to put these principles into practice at your company today.

Back the mid-2000s, however, these principles were just coming into focus for the eBay analytics team as we tried to make good on our mandate to stand up architectures commensurate with the newly critical role analytics needed to play in our company's survival. Some of these principles, in fact, became clear only in hindsight.

While our team was highly motivated and the company brass was on board with the effort, we still found ourselves at square one in many ways when it came to working with eBay's business users.

Quite frankly, the subjective experience was that our processes and methodologies had given us a bad reputation, and we weren't seen internally as good partners. In many ways, we had some of the most capable systems on Earth; but business users were running away from us for all the reasons we've laid out in this book so far about the requirements and ticket-driven status quo.

We realized we had to deliver solutions that not only helped the company, but also fit into the ways people naturally wanted to work so that IT collaboration stopped seeming like a chore for them. We chose a few key projects to turn things around.

One effort involved setting up collaborative platforms that became known first as data labs and, later, as the DataHub. A precursor to the Sentient Enterprise's LinkedIn for Analytics approach today, the

DataHub we created in the mid-2000s allowed eBay analysts to post interesting discoveries and correlations, with other eBay colleagues able to query the DataHub for tagged entries based on their areas of interest. People could add comments, follow a discussion, or link to certain groups focused on a specific tool or initiative. We designed the DataHub to allow safe experimentation; users could not just read analyst reports, but also manipulate charts and graphs as needed without messing up the data itself.

On another front, the eBay analytics team stepped up to help their vice president of Internet marketing sharpen the company's online advertising. Specifically, we needed to build analytics and instrument our website to capture and trace customer activity and outcomes on a very minute level—clickstream and other granular activity involving the behavioral data that we'll discuss more fully in Chapter 4. In the process, we reaped better insights than you could ever get from conducting customer surveys and similar customer relationship management (CRM) research.

As background, most customers never complain or respond to surveys; they just walk away and spend their money elsewhere if they're not happy. The analytics we built for the marketing team helped look beyond what customers say (or don't say) and examine their actual behavior with systematic precision. This can clarify friction points in the customer experience, and, in our case, it helped us understand overall customer behavior and preferences so we could use that knowledge to sharpen our targeted online marketing.

A final eBay example to share involves an analytics solution to optimize efficiencies in our data infrastructure around the world. We had built our reputation around capacity and reliability; now we needed analytics to preserve all that while boosting efficiency behind the scenes. To do this, we looked beyond immediate operations and metrics and charted performance over a three-month period.

This data allowed us to optimize server usage (we made changes in server deployment, load balance, and data traffic) to make operations more efficient to the point where 12,000 servers were able to do the work of what 15,000 servers had done before. Keep in mind this was back in 2008, right when the economic recession was hitting.

Analytics helped position eBay to survive that downturn by fulfilling capacity with a fraction of the infrastructure we had once needed.

We hope these examples show how taking an agile and collaborative approach to designing and building analytics architectures will help your company survive and compete in constantly changing and highly competitive markets. We were particularly pleased to see that eBay itself now references the Sentient Enterprise in an "Extreme Analytics @ eBay" presentation the company has been delivering at major events and conferences.

In the chapters to come, we'll use real-world examples like this wherever possible to explain what happens in the Sentient Enterprise's five stages, and how these innovations are already making a difference for real companies. The Sentient Enterprise is all about harvesting insights from experimentation, pilot projects, and lessons learned so we can understand and replicate agile success stories across industries—and at scale.

Agile and at scale. Bringing those two concepts together is, indeed, our key priority in presenting this book. You'll find plenty of books about agile ventures and entrepreneurial projects; there are also plenty of books on the shelf dealing with large-scale organizational management issues. In putting forth *The Sentient Enterprise*, we are bringing the two worlds together in ways you can model and replicate for success in your own company. The next five chapters (3 to 7) serve as your road map through the five stages of this capability maturity model. Our first stop is the Agile Data Platform.

CHAPTER 3

The Agile Data Platform

exas-based Dell, Inc. has thrived by skillfully adapting to business and consumer needs over more than three decades. By 2017, Dell was ranked as the world's largest privately held technology company and the United States' fourth largest private company, with revenues of $72 billion and a global workforce of more than 140,000 people. Like all large firms, Dell has found ways to scale operations globally, but not without significant data management challenges along the way.

"It came to a head for us when we set up global manufacturing processes and infrastructure," says Dell's vice president for enterprise services and order experience, Jennifer Felch. As Jennifer began telling us the story of Dell's initial push to aggregate global manufacturing data across all functions and regions into one master environment for reporting and analytics, the struggle she described sounded strikingly similar to the data drift, duplication, and other pain points we first highlighted in Chapter 1.

"At one point, we'd have a number of teams that were pulling data, doing analytics in their own data cubes, and then getting into meetings with each other and discussing why their data didn't match up," she told us in an interview. "People were taking data and it never came back. They would create reports, but that data never came back as shared data. Our number-one priority was to make the data transparent, accessible, and consistent as our company grew."

"Scaling is the forcing function for standardizing and becoming as efficient and accurate as possible with your data," Jennifer summarized. "We knew we had to find a solution." We'll take a closer look at that solution a little later in this chapter. But first, we need to understand just how common this challenge is as large organizations grow and scale operations.

RETAINING AGILITY AT SCALE

For most companies, bringing the Sentient Enterprise vision to life involves a wholesale makeover in how data is managed and manipulated as the organization grows in size and complexity. It's what we've been calling "change management on steroids" and something Siemens Mobility's Gerhard Kress considers "change management on all sides."

"Change management is the key lever. You have to help everyone understand what analytics means and what these data points can do

FIVE STAGES

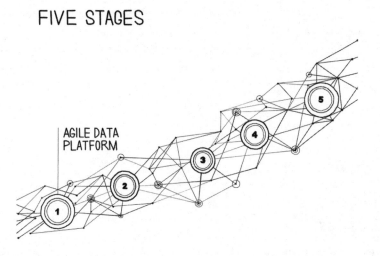

AGILE DATA
PLATFORM

for them," Gerhard told us. "In our case, we have to take engineers—who've spent years designing and creating a standing product—with us on the journey to understand how data helps us all become even better. And you have to connect them with all these young data scientists that come from university and want to rock the world.

"Getting all these people together to provide the best service for the customer is essential," he summarized. "And I think, without change management on all sides, there's nowhere you can make that happen." For Gerhard and most other technology executives, a key task is to get the whole organization on a much more agile footing with data.

For that, we set up the Agile Data Platform, the first of the five stages in the Sentient Enterprise journey. Here, we are going to apply a number of agile methodologies and systems to data and analytics, striking some careful balances along the way. We want to give users freedom to iterate on data without having to make copies of that data. We must get rid of excessive governance barriers without opening the floodgates to Wild West anarchy. We need effortless movement of information without turning our architectures into a collapsing house of cards of data drift and duplication. Above all, we have to give centralized access to data for decentralized experiments on use cases in a way that doesn't pollute the whole system with experiment-driven artifacts and error.

In order to be sustainable, this transformation to an Agile Data Platform must involve the right combination of people, processes, and technology. You can't just focus on one of these in isolation. You need to address everything—from organizational culture and processes to the architectures and governance that define how we store, share, analyze, and manipulate data for competitive advantage. So where do we start?

RETHINKING WATERFALL METHODOLOGIES

Near the top of our to-do list is to move beyond so-called waterfall methodologies that have dominated IT projects for decades. The approach gets its name from the steady downward flow of progress (like a waterfall) through distinct phases like conception, initiation, analysis, design, construction, testing, production, implementation, and maintenance. It's a stately progression where requirements are laid out up front, even though these requirements may end up changing along the way.

Unfortunately, waterfall methodologies have difficulty handling changes midstream; this is a chief criticism of the approach and the reason it's not agile. Clients may not know exactly what they want until they see a working prototype or system, and then their requirements could change as a result. Designers may encounter new or unforeseen problems at that point as well. Either way, waterfall development brings delays and extra cost for redesign, redevelopment, and retesting.

Many have tried incremental improvements, like introducing some degree of overlap between waterfall stages. But others have sought more wholesale changes. The U.S. Department of Defense (DoD), for instance, has stated its preference against waterfall-type methodologies in favor of more iterative and incremental development models. The DoD is on the right path here, and organizations that succeed in taking analytics beyond waterfall to more agile approaches will find they can supercharge their analytics capabilities and the value these capabilities reap for the enterprise.

This change can also streamline collaboration between IT and the rest of the organization. Waterfall strategies and their glacial time lines are a big part of why so many IT departments have gotten a bad reputation in their companies as slow and uncooperative partners. Many now see the need for a basic rethinking of how to structure IT product development. Nowhere is the need greater than in the fast-changing world of analytics.

AGILE ANALYTICS

The Agile Data Platform relies on our analytics professionals finding better ways to configure projects and collaborate with the rest of the company. Fortunately, the majority of people building agile systems around analytics today have the benefit of more and more templates and frameworks now available to help guide their work. We happen to be big fans of agile development methodologies like Scrum.

Chapter 8 includes more details on how to implement and work with Scrum, but we'll discuss it here as a prime example of the kind of agile development and project management platform that helps drive analytic change throughout the organization.

Scrum lays out several key roles designed to support an agile environment. The product owner represents external stakeholders and is generally considered to be the voice of the customer, even if that customer is an internal colleague in another department who needs an analytic solution. Rather than deliver complicated requirements documents, the product owner generally drafts user stories or other customer-centric narratives to define and prioritize needs. The development team is responsible for doing the actual work on analysis, design, development, documentation, and implementation. Though such teams are often small—typically 10 people or fewer—they are cross-functional and collectively possess all the skills necessary to do the job.

Then there is a Scrum master, who is responsible for troubleshooting and removing impediments. The Scrum master is neither a proxy for the customer nor a traditional team lead or project manager. The job is more like a facilitator who ensures the team follows the agreed Scrum processes and acts as a buffer between the team and any distracting influences.

Scrum's overall framework is loose and dynamic enough to act as an "exposure model" to quickly identify problems and innovative ways to overcome them. But loose doesn't mean undisciplined. Indeed, while the word itself is derived from the scrum of rugby play—as in the "disorderly struggle or fight" in Merriam-Webster's definition—there's really a highly organized process that's under way in a Scrum project. Things may seem disorderly on the surface, but what you're seeing is a proven and successful framework for constant feedback, strategic adjustments, and course correction that has been adopted broadly for projects in education, marketing, operations, and other settings.

This flexible methodology was first conceived for software product development, but Scrum also happens to be extremely well suited for analytics. That's because the same flexibility built into the methodology to handle requirements churn from software customers is also useful for handling the ever-changing conditions analytics professionals discover as we use data in new ways and tweak capabilities.

Ultimately, however, your agile project management platform must thoroughly replace, not rest on top of, the same old waterfall procedures. Otherwise, you get what's called "waterscrum" or "scrummerfall"; and while the nicknames may be humorous, the results—in terms of lost opportunities for innovation and competitive advantage—are not. You cannot simply reverse engineer agility. Platforms like Scrum are just part of that larger blueprint for making true agility happen throughout the organization.

Another key part of this blueprint is the self-service ethic we discussed in Chapter 1. It is no use having Scrum or other agile platforms without self-service tools to accompany them. Unfortunately, many infrastructures are set up for a waterfall methodology. Things like ticketing systems with service-level agreements (SLAs) of seven days or more are all too common and will prohibit Scrum from becoming successful. Agile development and self-service tooling have to go hand in hand. And in the Sentient Enterprise, the way this happens is through a new kind of data mart.

SPREADING AGILITY COMPANY-WIDE WITH THE VIRTUAL DATA MART

Creating the Agile Data Platform involves pivoting from what you'd consider traditional data warehouse structures and methodologies to a more balanced and decentralized framework that's built for agility. Hosting your data in enterprise data warehouses (EDWs) certainly isn't agile; but we've already learned that it doesn't help matters when we build siloed data marts that sabotage your systems with error and anarchy.

Bear in mind that data marts are not found just in legacy technology. In fact, most data marts created today are built with SQL, NoSQL, databases, file systems or similar technologies. Open source or not, legacy or not—if a system creates an extra copy of data or is a nonintegrated silo of data, then it's a data mart. The biggest silos of all have actually been built on the likes of Hadoop, as the ability to scale has driven their sizes into the petabyte scale.

As said before, any sustainable plan for improvement requires that we reimagine how people, processes, and technology all come together around data. Remember how we met the well-intentioned financial analyst in Chapter 1 who didn't want to wait 18 months for IT to help him set up a data research project on asset allocation? His unfortunate choice was to build his own data mart—a collection of copies from his company's broader data infrastructure. It was his Wild West solution that gave him quick—and wrong—results as the data values and accuracy drifted every time he copied his own little slice of the company's data and manipulated it.

To get agile throughout the organization and make it sustainable, we need to retain this convenient, self-service sandbox concept of a data mart or data lab, but build it in a way where it doesn't pollute the larger data ecosystem. The answer is what we call the virtual data mart (VDM), which replicates many of the conditions that lure colleagues to the traditional data mart (perceived agility and minimal red tape) without the pitfalls (data drift, duplication, and error).

At the beginning of this chapter, we highlighted the need to give centralized access to data for decentralized use cases, and this is exactly what VDMs do. They let users rapidly access production data along with their own data to quickly execute their own specific use cases. But these activities do not alter the production data itself. If you're using a VDM, you can safely experiment and build prototypes by plugging into existing data and capturing and refining your current data templates and rules.

Multiple users across the organization are creating VDMs simultaneously in real time. As a result, you get accurate and clean data that is still flexible because anyone in the enterprise can request and analyze that data, anytime and anywhere. The VDMs must be easy to use or else they'll represent just another hurdle. That's why the VDM sits on top, or inside, of existing platforms where we have all the data. As a user, the moment you provision that VDM (or sandbox, data lab, or whatever you want to call it), you already see all data that you're allowed to see.

Whatever you're certified for, your access to data within that context should be like an open book. This is a key point: Once IT covers basic needs for certification, it's time to get out of the judgment business. That's why we recommend companies designate a certain amount of storage (100 or 200 gigabytes, let's say) on a no-questions-asked basis. Ideally, this kind of self-service provisioning can happen right away, in five minutes or less.

A VIRTUAL DATA MART (BY ANY OTHER NAME) IN ACTION

In case you think we're talking just in hypotheticals, let's take a closer look at Dell and the challenge faced by Jennifer Felch and her colleagues. When the company was founded by Michael Dell in 1984, it was initially a pure hardware vendor. Dell was an early pioneer in supply chain management and electronic commerce—particularly the build-to-order or configure-to-order approach to manufacturing.

Dell has since expanded into IT services, enterprise solutions, software, and client solutions, selling everything from personal computers, servers, and data storage devices to network switches, software programs, computer peripherals, cameras, TVs, and printers. This growth led to the daunting challenge Jennifer Felch shared with us at the start of this chapter.

As vice president for enterprise services and order experience, Jennifer found herself with the mission-critical task of aggregating data for reporting and analytics on global manufacturing into one master environment. That environment had to account for all manufacturing functions and regions around the world—and it all had to be done while keeping data transparent, accessible, and consistent across the organization!

Dell solved the issue by developing the company's own version of what we've been calling the virtual data mart (VDM). "We have a lab environment now, with 25 business-supported active labs," said Jennifer. "This environment doesn't change the master, and it also doesn't take data away into another level in some cube where there's no return path.

"So now our teams have access to all of that data; they get to play with data and figure out what makes sense," Jennifer continued. "Once there's agreement on the definitions, the meanings, even the calculations—once we reach a point where we can collectively say something like 'Hey, this seems to be the best way to measure this particular KPI across the board'—we can put that back into the common data environment and everybody has access to it.

"The takeaway for us was pretty clear," Jennifer summarized. "Scaling was the forcing function that said to us, 'You're going to have to change your processes.' It's not that we had poor practices before. It's just that, in the shift to leveraging more global processes and infrastructure, we needed to adjust the way we worked with data as well."

TIME BOXING

Dell's experience shows how powerful VDMs can be. Part of Dell's success, however—and that of any company taking this approach— lies in how the VDM environment is managed over time. Almost by definition, these data labs are temporary tools for experimentation and discovery. That means we need to slide in some kind of governance so that, over the long term, we don't end up with many thousands of data marts that people may not need or use anymore.

VDMs don't simply disappear when you're done with them. How can you keep them from accumulating like digital deadwood that takes up valuable space on your systems? The answer is to time box, a tried-and-true method for allocating capacity where it's needed most. Here's how it works:

Make it easy for people in your company to provision a VDM, but designate access for a limited amount of time—typically 30, 60, or 90 days. These are reasonable time frames for anyone running analytics experiments to either hit pay dirt (or at least find a promising lead) or else give up. You can easily build in automatic notifications when VDM access is about to expire; send an e-mail alert 10 or 15 days before system expiration, for example.

Within that notification, make it simple for a user who needs more time to just click a link and extend access for another month or two. If folks are onto something, they'll ask for more time. If not, they'll ignore the e-mail alerts and won't care if their VDM disappears.

Throughout this process, it's critically important that you devote enough capacity to support the VDM environment. Even with automatic processes that purge unused or unneeded experiments, you still have to devote a significant amount of capacity for the many data marts currently in use. This need will grow as you rack up wins and the approach catches on throughout the company.

Our point here is that you can't just turn on a sandbox environment. You may ultimately need as much as 30 to 50 percent of your company's system capacity allocated for this kind of experimentation; most companies today have only zero to 5 percent of their capacity devoted to such uses. Without devoting the needed capacity, it'd be like launching a severely understaffed call center, with all the dysfunction and frustration you'd expect to go along with that.

FEWER REQUIREMENTS, MORE PROTOTYPES

When set up correctly, your VDM system is a cornerstone in the Agile Data Platform—a self-service environment for innovation where people basically self-select when they're onto something. It's easy to keep track of those in the company who are asking for more time and have likely gone beyond the stage of having an initial prototype.

You see how innovation remains seamless and hassle-free throughout this process. We are not talking waterfall-style requirements here. It's more a natural way of observing who is doing what with data, and finding strategic ways for IT to help bring a solution to maturity when a team is making progress on a prototype. So what do we put in place of those old waterfall requirements documents?

The answer is to institute what we call a "speedboat" or "fast-track" approach, and it's a very simple one. It basically means that anyone who gets to the point of having a working prototype can then enter into a fast-track program of IT assistance to fortify and replicate the prototype for production use. As we'll see more fully in Chapter 6, cloud and so-called DevOps resources can facilitate this approach.

It's a "start small, scale fast" approach with no room, and no need, for waterfall requirements. That's because prototypes are much more useful than any requirements document could ever be. They give you a highly focused scope set of algorithms and outputs versus the broad definitions you see in waterfall methodologies. Prototypes usually result in basic dashboards and visualizations, and they represent a ton of questions already asked and answered on the experimenter's part, any one of which may have prompted a "back to the drawing board" moment in a waterfall system of development.

We can tell you from experience that one working prototype is worth 100 requirements documents. That's because a lot of the work is already done, so IT can focus on maturing the prototype into a production application. Rather than dealing with massive projects, your analytics teams are now working on many different small prototypes, nudging the best ones along to maturity and company-wide value.

Taken together, these prototypes make up a seedbed for innovation. And the time frame for realizing whether a particular prototype should be shelved, discarded, or taken further into production is very short, typically four to six weeks. You will find that many candidates will indeed get abandoned along the way in this "fail fast" environment. But other prototypes will make it to maturity and create real value for the company for a fraction of the time and expense that come with waterfall methodologies.

ANALYTICS ON ANALYTICS

So far, we've laid out a dynamic and innovative self-service environment to become agile around analytics. To get the most value out of the process, however, it's very important to put the instrumentation in place so you're able to say, "Not only can I support self-service, but I can govern it."

Precisely because we're letting people experiment and build their own prototypes and pilot systems before we send our architects to intervene and assist, we need a mechanism to analyze and reconstruct the steps our colleagues took in reaching the point of a successful prototype.

This is important, because people don't usually keep track of every step they've taken, and they shouldn't have to. Whether the goal is to troubleshoot or tweak, reconstruct or recommend, architects must have an unobtrusive way of logging and replaying every interaction in real time as people are working in their data labs—and retrieving that information after the fact to review where key decisions and insights were made.

In the Sentient Enterprise, we call this "analytics on analytics," and it involves setting up our VDM environment so that every interaction in every sandbox and data lab is captured by default. We may not know in the moment which interactions will become useful in retrospect. But every interaction is documented so we can have it all at our disposal as we look at the success stories and piece together which data and analytic approaches helped contribute to them. Think of it as your clickstream of analytical usage.

Doing analytics on analytics gives us a granular understanding of what worked and what didn't work as prototypes and analytics models came into being. In logging what everyone has done, we can review any part of the development process, and even replay events in sequence to get a dynamic picture of what happened over a period of time (e.g., "Let's look at those final two weeks of prototype development and take a closer look at where this dashboard glitch was coming from before we fixed it"). An added benefit of this approach is that we are primarily looking at what has worked, since most of the failed approaches died in the sandbox stage and never reached the point of functioning prototype and IT intervention.

MAKING IT REAL WITH THE LAYERED DATA ARCHITECTURE

All the strategies we've laid out so far in this chapter will help us become more agile with data. But none of them can really work if we don't have solid data architectures to support and undergird this agile environment. Otherwise the whole discussion of agility is just window dressing. If there's no "there" there, people will simply revert to water-fall methodologies.

Remember how our definition of agility in the Introduction centered on decomposing problems into smaller ones so they're easier to solve and collaborate around? The architecture we need must act as a decomposition framework for data itself, a classification tool that handles data in its many forms (raw, loosely or tightly coupled, etc.).

Beginning with the raw, atomic data, our architecture must render information at multiple levels of complexity and assign lanes and roles so we can overlay many different kinds of users onto the same data, and do so in the contexts that these multiple users are familiar with. In the Sentient Enterprise, we call this the Layered Data Architecture (LDA).

LAYERED DATA ARCHITECTURE

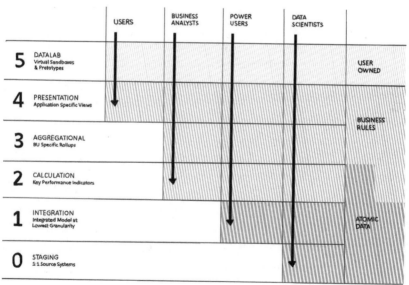

You'll see multiple mentions of the LDA throughout this book, since it's a central framework that comes into play throughout the five stages of the Sentient Enterprise journey.

The lowest staging layer contains atomic data that is stored in its original fidelity from source systems. In this layer, data should reflect as closely as possible the source system representation, and that includes lineage of data types and structures. Dates or financial data, for instance, must not become just text, or else you've just allowed the very first breakage of lineage to occur.

The staging layer can be accessed by the most technical data engineers or data scientists in your company. Keep in mind that this layer is not the same as a stand-alone data lake. Instead, Layer 0 needs to be part of the overall platform, capable of scaling in size, in complexity, and—crucially—in concurrency. You cannot build a stand-alone version of Layer 0 as a data lake, in other words, and have it be limited to a few dozen concurrent jobs accessing data in it.

Your staging layer must be enterprise scale, with hundreds of thousands of users and processes simultaneously accessing and processing data from it. The same data will have to be used in multiple ways (by customers, segments, products, hierarchies, internal versus external views, and financial or marketing use cases).

The higher up you go in the LDA, however, the more predefined structure you have, and the more intelligible your analytics become to more people in your enterprise. By the time you get to the aggregation layer, your business users can comfortably access and categorize data sets by customer attribute, location, revenue, or any number of criteria that might be familiar and useful to them.

Still further up, the presentation layer is the most structured and predefined. This is where various groups can access numbers through different interfaces, but still sees the same data. Think of the presentation layer as the published API to your data—mainly structured, version controlled, maintained for backward compatibility, and made available to any user or application authorized to access parts of it. Finally, the data lab is the user-owned sandbox that supports experimentation and self-service. These are the VDMs we've been talking about at length in this chapter.

The LDA is the foundation of the Agile Data Platform. It's the engine that drives our frictionless, self-service analytics model that gives centralized access for decentralized use cases. It's what helps us all collaborate around data while still controlling access and governance. Remember our definition of agility as decomposing problems or systems to make them manageable? Think of the LDA as a decomposition framework for data and processes.

DRIVING CHANGE IN THE AUTO INDUSTRY

An LDA approach is certainly at work for General Motors. "We're rapidly accelerating the acquisition and colocation of data," said GM's Brett Vermette, whom we first met in Chapter 1. "We're taking what you'd call integrated data and really denormalizing it, making it readily available in a form that's easily consumable by 80 percent or some majority of people who need it at various levels.

"Much of the data acquired during the early days of our EDW program is very integrated and structured to help reduce replication and ensure integrity of keys across tables," Brett explained. "So what we're doing is working to try to combine some of that data, reduce the number of joins that are necessary to make that data useful, and put in some data structures that people can relatively easily consume."

When we first caught up with Brett in Chapter 1, he was talking about GM's self-imposed analytics overhaul to bring order to hundreds of data marts. During our interview, he shared a few more recollections on that successful, company-wide effort:

"In a matter of months, we quickly ramped up from a small handful of data warehousing professionals to several hundred. We brought in people with deep history in the space. We did an initial six-week study to inventory our landscape, built a road map for technology deployment, [and made] staffing plans. The study also helped identify more than 200 data marts all over the company.

"From our perspective, data marts are bad—they're legacy analytics platforms and repositories that are often outdated and definitely not widely available or integrated. So what we're really trying to do is consolidate our data marts across the company. We frankly weren't surprised at the number of data marts we found. If you think back to the history of GM as a company, it had been a loosely connected conglomerate of organizations like Cadillac, Chevrolet, Buick, Oldsmobile, and Pontiac; there was our truck and bus group, and we also had Saturn. Each of those parts of the organization operated independently from an IT standpoint.

"So we have a long history of challenges involving siloed applications and the need for more integration across functional disciplines. We decided to bring all that data together and try to provide a unified foundation for people to look at the data we use to run the company much more holistically. In some cases, you need a high degree of curation, governance, management, and integration of data for usable results that give a viewpoint across the entire company. Other solutions may be just fine with less integration and little or no data curation. We're shifting to a mind-set of 'All data has value, regardless of the level of curation.'

"Our first solutions involved taking some sets of data and making it more widely available. We took 'dynamic vehicle test' data—the testing that's first done on a vehicle before it leaves the plant—and integrated that data across the plants to make it more readily available to more people in the company. In a similar way, we built capabilities to better share and analyze financial data on vehicle profitability."

From there, Brett says GM's data transformation has gone on to support numerous sectors and stakeholders throughout the business. "You can point in almost any direction and see the benefits," he told us, citing several examples. "As a shareholder, you're seeing improved decision making on profitability and other analyses; in marketing, our call center operations are much more proactive; and vehicle safety, performance, and quality control are augmented as well."

REMEMBERING THE BIG PICTURE

Never forget—and it must seem like our mantra by now—agility requires that you optimize how people, processes, and technology all convene around data. It is a constant balancing act, and any efforts you make in one area will be undercut if you don't also address the other two as well. You need to consider all three factors when implementing better systems in your organization. In fact, our implementation-focused Chapter 8 features a bit more detail on how your company can put into practice some of the people, processes, and technology initiatives discussed so far.

Particularly on the people front, don't underestimate your company's need for training and guidance. Offer good internal professional services that manage engagement with prototyping teams. Assign architects and data scientists as advisers to these prototype teams, and have your advisers consider physically moving their offices to where such teams are working.

Get used to making the case for change to colleagues who may not immediately understand. Most people are terrified of failure, so you have to help them understand the "fail fast" mind-set that goes along with speed boat development of multiple prototypes coming out of the VDM ecosystem. You may also find yourself explaining to skeptics why it's important to devote as much as half of your company's system capacity to these data labs.

Striking the right balance also involves recognizing that, for all the flexibility we get from VDMs and postwaterfall iterative and incremental development models, agile does not totally replace the need for waterfall or centralized architecture functions in your organization. Yes, you need to start small, scale fast, and not try to boil the ocean by applying new innovations to the whole company right away. But you'll eventually need to leverage centralized systems to create fully mature solutions and spread them to other parts of the company. Centralized architectures and centralized applications are hallmarks of any major enterprise, and you absolutely need them in the mix at some point in the maturation process.

Once you open up data access with the Agile Data Platform and its LDA, people will be free to explore the data and ask deeper questions about customer life cycles and relationships. This presents new possibilities, but also new challenges. That's where the next stage in the Sentient Enterprise journey comes in: the Behavioral Data Platform.

CHAPTER **4**

The Behavioral
Data Platform

Think back to a generation ago, when the economy was focused squarely on products and transactions: products sold, prices paid, and perhaps basic records on product returns or warranty repairs. In those bygone days, pretty much everything about what the customer thought, felt, believed, or doubted remained anecdotal and shared mostly person to person—by phone, letters, or in face-to-face conversations with employees at the store.

Now think of a very different scenario that plays out every day at a modern company like eBay: As the American multinational e-commerce giant supports activity around 800 million auction listings at any given time, a sophisticated Customer DNA database is parsing online activity—patterns around browsing, bidding, buying, spending, reviews, and numerous other factors—to build comprehensive, data-driven profiles of each customer for insight at the individual and aggregate levels.

The Customer DNA is, in many ways, the backbone of the company. Data is used to get a complete view of customers, including their attitudes, behaviors, demographics, and interests, as well as their value to eBay. The system looks at cart data, watch data, and cross-shop behavior, and how much of these and other activities is happening on desktop versus mobile. Ultimately, this Customer DNA environment creates a unified view of the customer base and all the individual variations for some very powerful insights into customer behaviors.

As we'll explore in this chapter, today's economy is now driven by a much deeper understanding of customer experiences and behaviors. We'll see how business success today requires us to leverage the agility groundwork we laid in Chapter 3 to create the right Behavioral Data Platform—Stage 2 in the Sentient Enterprise journey—so we can understand and manage these customer experiences and behaviors.

Decades ago, however, customer sentiment—what people thought and felt about a transaction—remained an afterthought to the transaction itself. This scenario worked perfectly well in a twentieth century dominated by revolutionary new products that created new needs and markets for an eager buying public. The advent of telephones, mass-produced automobiles, kitchen appliances, televisions, personal computers, and other items drove the economy. Even at production scale, the focus remained very much on the product. Customers were wowed by the object itself, and consumer financing options helped

FIVE STAGES

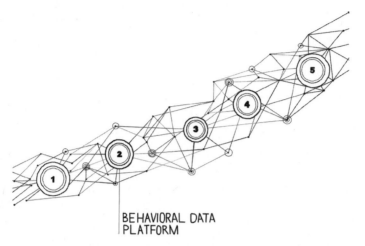

BEHAVIORAL DATA
PLATFORM

keep the transactions going. Growth relied on making more and more products for more and more people to purchase.

This was the time before big data and e-commerce, before Yelp and Facebook. Comparison shopping was resource intensive, with savvy shoppers needing to make the effort to drive from store to store, search newspaper ads, or comb through back issues of *Consumer Reports*. And even then, customers' knowledge of the best product didn't guarantee they could get their hands on it in an era before Amazon, eBay, and free same-day shipping. Today, however, everything is different!

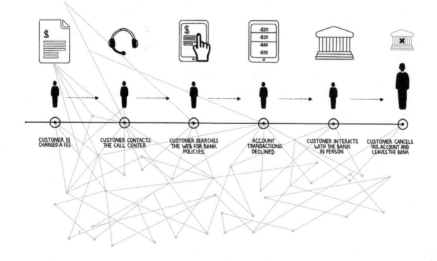

PERSONALIZED—IF NOT PERSONAL—INTERACTION

As customers, we have more convenience and more choices; and we've become more demanding because of this. The nature of competition has therefore shifted in a fundamental way: The customer experience is now paramount, and a company's ability to create a good one is now a chief differentiator for success.

To further complicate matters, the days of vast new markets and frequent unveilings of radically new products are mostly over. It's easier to create a great customer experience when it comes in the form of a radically new product (the iPhone's arrival is probably the latest major revolution, and that was a decade ago). These days, it's a more nuanced and difficult sell when you're operating in saturated markets. Today's companies typically find growth in adding services, incremental improvements, or—as anyone can tell from watching the never-ending price wars in the cellular market—luring new customers from competitors.

As an added challenge to business, the same digital and globally linked environment that elevated customer demands has also complicated our ability to satisfy these demands. The personalization we may see at the local level is completely missing at the global scale. And while today's customers have learned not to expect a face-to-face interaction, they do expect a customized and easy experience. They expect convenience.

This consumer demand for convenience has replaced personal contact as a priority, and it's a complicated thing to provide. Customers know their experience today may not be personal, but they demand that it feel personalized with things like good algorithms for product suggestions, knowledgeable tech or product support, hassle-free shipping, and seamless omnichannel integration of the online and brick-and-mortar experience. When there's a problem, they want a better customer experience at all touch points, including one-call resolution and streamlined, multichannel processes for returns and refunds.

Amid all this change is a lesson that any company with even a prayer of competing and surviving in today's economy needs to learn: With the customer experience now a top priority, the only way to leverage it is to track and optimize customer behaviors and the data that reflect these behaviors.

NEW MEASURES FOR SUCCESS, BUILT ON BEHAVIORAL DATA

As a result, all levels of the enterprise need to shift from transactional to behavioral thinking. CXOs in particular must focus more fully on behavioral issues like customer satisfaction and sentiment versus a pure revenue and profit mind-set. This evolution of understanding involves getting C-suite leaders to think in customer-centric terms and realize that a stronger bond between the enterprise and its customers will ultimately have a positive impact on revenue and profits in the mid to long term.

That's why successful leaders are learning to embrace key performance indicators based on buyer sentiment. We happen to be big believers in a key performance indicator known as the Net Promoter Score, which helps correlate the strength of customer relationships with company revenue and growth.

Created in 2003 as an alternative to more traditional customer satisfaction research, the Net Promoter Score measures customers' willingness to recommend a company's products or services to others. The score index ranges from –100 (everyone is a detractor) to +100 (everyone is a promoter). Obviously you want to be in positive territory, and a score of +80 or more is considered to be very good.

In a preview of what's to come, keep in mind that as we reach the end state where "sentient" algorithms are making the decisions, the Net Promoter Score may involve customers rating their satisfaction with how algorithms—not necessarily people—are doing their jobs. Nowhere is this more evident, and more imminent, than with the advent of self driving taxis and ride-hailing services.

Right now, for instance, riders using Lyft or Uber are essentially providing an implicit Net Promoter Score every time they give ratings for their drivers and the overall trip experience. But algorithms will soon change that. As Lyft partners with General Motors to put thousands of self-driving electric cars on the road as early as 2018, and as Uber continues its testing of autonomous vehicles in cities like Pittsburgh, PA, and Tempe, AZ, the time is near when such a Net Promoter Score will involve rider assessments not of people, but of the algorithms responsible for operating the vehicle.

Did I get carsick? Was I scared by a sudden move? Did my "driver" seem confused and stuck at that four-way intersection? Such questions will be directed not toward a human behind the wheel, but at the array of complex digital systems working together to drive the car. Equally complex will be the remedy for negative Net Promoter Scores. No longer will you, as the service provider, be able to simply fire the driver; instead, you'll have to analyze what may be dozens of complex, concurrent systems.

Keep in mind that this pressure to apply new measures of customer sentiment to a new technology will be happening in the midst of immediate and intense market competition: At least three major auto manufacturers (General Motors, Ford, and Volvo) have already made clear their intention to put self-driving taxi or ride hailing fleet vehicles on public roads in just the next few years. (We'll learn much more in Chapter 7 about self-driving cars, since they serve as a microcosm for the analytics-fueled "sentience" we're ultimately hoping to achieve throughout the entire enterprise.)

Now and in the future, transactions will remain important. But without a deeper understanding of customers and the behaviors that will bring them to you and keep them loyal over time, you're ignoring reality and sacrificing long-term growth for short-term revenue and profit. Customers are not like products that you can stock up and sell. You don't possess customers; you retain them!

When we understand the value of the customer experience, and the behaviors that serve as markers and artifacts of this experience, we begin to see how analytics needs to be completely different. We must learn to drive decisions based on the behavioral patterns and the flood of behavioral data.

Behavioral data is all those events and data points in between or across transactions. Suddenly, it's less about counting the products you sold this week versus last week. You now also have to look at behaviors and outcomes to answer questions like: What are people saying and doing? How are they likely to act in the future, and what are our next logical steps? How can I make the most of every touch point that I have? How do I get feedback if the customer was happy? What if my customer is angry? How do I turn a bad situation into a good one, and how quickly can I make that happen?

We need to find and interpret the data to answer these questions. Whether you're studying the behavior of individuals or systems as a whole, you must look for patterns of behavior that lead to new insights. For example, we might look at the key behavioral steps that lead to customer acquisition and up-sell or cross-sell. We can also take readings of sensors around the world, opening up analytical capabilities for the Internet of Things (IoT).

Behavioral data lets us dig deeply into the areas where transactional information can't begin to take us: Yes, John bought a Ford Mustang; we can see that transaction. But what about all the other people who *didn't* buy? Were there some people who were on the path to buying a Mustang but who changed their mind at some point? Where was that point, and what was the reason? How can I learn to spot nonbuying behavior like this in the future? When and how should I intervene to get them back on the path to purchasing?

The laundry list of questions—all of them solvable only through close examination of behavioral data—will vary from company to company, depending on the industry, products, and services involved.

"We are always looking at subscriber growth," said Grace Hwang, executive director for business intelligence and advanced analytics at Verizon Wireless. "Where can we find them? What pricing levels and bundles make the most sense for which customers? When we change pricing and promotion, how will that affect our position against competition—and what demographic, geographic, or other variables should we consider?"

LEVERAGING BEHAVIORAL DATA FOR REAL-WORLD BUSINESS CHALLENGES

We first met Grace Hwang in our Introduction, where she shared Verizon's Company Credo and its mission to leverage economy of scale while remaining nimble and proactive. As we'll see shortly, Verizon's mission has been a successful one in no small part because the company always pegs its efforts to real-world outcomes. "It ultimately comes down to staying relevant," Grace told us. "You've got to stay relevant to your customer."

Staying relevant in today's fast-changing world is an achievement for any company; but it's a particularly striking one for large, established organizations. Remember our previous chapter's discussion of Dell's agility efforts around global manufacturing? That's just one piece of a company-wide effort to not just streamline its own operations but to position it to compete, even dominate, in today's economy. A case in point is Dell's $67 billion initiative to purchase fellow tech giant EMC and meet, as the *New York Times* put it, "the challenge of integrating a fellow old-line tech company in a world in which new technologies have already upset other venerable names."

Verizon gained similar headlines of its own with the July 2016 announcement that it would buy Yahoo!'s core Internet properties for more than $4.8 billion in cash. Here is Verizon, a large and established company with roots going back many decades to the old Bell system, which is now thriving to the point where it is able to buy an Internet pioneer. What's more, given Yahoo!'s run through six CEOs in less than a decade, Verizon is positioning itself to succeed where previous efforts to right the troubled company have fallen short.

What's behind this and other achievements, like Verizon's 2015 acquisition of America Online (AOL), its position as the number one U.S. wireless operator, and its reputation for having the industry's lowest customer churn rate in the United States? In our opinion, powerful and proactive analytics fueled by behavioral data have played no small part. Major acquisitions and other big milestones of success are the culmination of countless instances of data-driven decisioning to predict trends, seize market opportunities, and navigate around or through the next crisis.

When asked, Verizon's Grace Hwang had no trouble bringing one such instance to mind. It was back in 2011, when Apple's iOS 5 update included the debut of iMessage, a free texting service that suddenly allowed iPhone users to sidestep carriers when texting between iOS devices, including other iPhones.

"That was a major change," Grace told us. "It was a huge deal at the time, because carriers made a lot of money from text messaging plans." Indeed, texting accounted for some $23 billion in revenue for carriers in 2011; Verizon Wireless alone was generating an estimated $7 billion, or about 12 percent of the company's total annual revenue, from text messaging.

"It was very short notice, and it was up to us to figure out, 'How can we get on a predictive curve?'" said Grace. "We had to ask, 'If all the Apple-to-Apple text messages go away, what will our customers do? How will they react when they don't see the same value in our text messaging plans anymore?'" Her company's use of analytics to find answers proactively speaks volumes about why Verizon enjoys the market dominance it does today:

"Before the iMessage release, we built a monitoring mechanism. The COO needed leading indicators and a sense of when to adjust our pricing so we're not hurting our business. We were saying, 'Okay, where can I see Apple-to-Apple messages—not penetrating privacy but using switch data and other ways to see, in aggregate, which messages are Apple to Apple, which others involve incoming texts from other carriers, and so forth?'

"We needed to be able to come to leadership with data and context that would then drive decisions in IT, marketing—everything—to be ready to shift our pricing focus to the metering of data and let go of voice and texting as the revenue sources we were used to. Ultimately, we were able to time when to switch pricing to unlimited talk and text, and what that pricing should be. The whole industry moved in that direction, but our job was to figure out how to do it best and fastest.

"This was a true predictive use case," Grace summarized. "We had to be proactive and find the right information and behaviors on a leading indicator basis. Ultimately, the metrics and impact were huge. You're talking tens of millions of dollars a year of potential loss had we not been proactive."

In the course of writing this book, we've found how this proactive use of data to tackle even the most daunting organizational challenges seems to be a signature strategy for top analytics practitioners and executives.

"I'm a huge football fan, so when I think of the chief data officer's charter, it's a lot like the 'pick six' opportunity you see out on the playing field when a quarterback throws a pass and there's an interception by a defender who is then able to run the ball into the end zone for a touchdown," said A. Charles Thomas, who at the time of his interview for this book was chief data officer at Wells Fargo, but is now chief data officer at General Motors. In the interview, Charles explained how the "pick six" applies to the analytic playbook.

"If your defense is only stopping plays, that's fine. But the bonus is to also generate points and find that opportunity to advance the team," Charles told us. "That's what you need to do with analytics:

you take what may be a challenging or defensive situation and find ways to turn the situation around into a winning scenario."

"It is important to use a wide variety of rich behavioral data—including speech to text, online feedback, account behavior, in-person interactions, and letters we receive—to do root cause analysis and get a good understanding of what any problems are. For instance, if you get complaints from customers about delays in receiving their credit cards in the mail, the data can help find similarities or trends within that complaint data; perhaps it's related to geography, the underwriting process, or something about the mailing addresses. This is how the data can help us not only identify common dynamics to any problem, but predict those dynamics moving forward.

"The ability to both understand and predict circumstances allows us to move forward proactively. You are then able to enhance our own processes internally and also reach out proactively to customers, often before they may even realize there's an issue. We can be the ones to alert them about the situation, and let them know how we're already fixing it for them. It takes a lot of coordination and collaboration around data within the organization. But if you can pull it off, these are the kind of 'pick six' opportunities that help turn a challenging scenario into one that can enhance your own operations and your relationship and trust with the customer—all of which can save money for the company."

BEHAVIORAL DATA IS EVERYWHERE

For the sake of clarity, we've so far been talking mostly in the context of consumer-facing goods and services. But keep in mind that this shift from transactional to behavioral data is an across-the-board upheaval that extends to industrial settings and how we work with machine and sensor data.

As we discussed in Chapter 2, the sensor-driven Internet of Things is revolutionizing our ability to index the world, predict future circumstances, and control future outcomes. We highlighted in that chapter the "black box" event data recorders in most new cars. The sensors inside are tracking the behaviors of both the car and the driver, capturing vehicle operations and driving habits to optimize performance, improve future engine design, or spot unsafe driving.

As another example, airline operators and manufacturers can now use the many sensors on a plane to measure and customize performance based on duty cycle. An aircraft used for cross-country routes may fly many miles with fewer takeoffs and landings; the opposite may be the case for the same kind of plane assigned to regional routes. In these situations, sensor data can help you make duty-specific adjustments to optimize safety and fuel efficiency.

Behavioral data and analytics extend to completely industrial settings as well, like what sensors can tell us about wind turbine performance, or wear and tear on oil exploration drill bits as they're exposed to various factors like heat, torque, and changes in rock composition.

The behavioral patterns allow us to better understand interactions. Humans shop, research, and interact with the company in countless ways. Machines perform and deliver different results based on their surroundings and conditions. We no longer just count or aggregate data points; we're connecting them in complex ways.

From industrial settings and fleet logistics to personal driving or shopping habits, behavioral data is the source of tremendously valuable insights for business. It shows patterns and context and helps us mature our analytics to the point where we can predict and prevent setbacks in anything from human buying habits to machine performance.

AGILE SYSTEMS FOR BEHAVIORAL DATA

Now that we've illustrated the tremendous opportunities that come with behavioral data, we're going to spend the rest of this chapter learning how to operationalize such data in the enterprise—how, in other words, to make the Behavioral Data Platform a reality in your organization. You'll remember from Chapter 1 that behavioral data involves tremendously large data volumes and varieties of information. That means our architectures and analytics must be able to handle the 10 to 100 times higher volumes and increased complexity involved.

The reason for all this data is that it makes up a vast landscape of information, within which lie patterns of activity representing the behaviors we've been talking about. It's not just statistics and bean counting. Instead we're looking for signals amid all the noise, and this requires many data points. We need an architecture that allows us to work in a wide-open field where there may be hundreds or thousands of clicks happening for every transaction.

An individual click during a sale is meaningless, just as an individual sensor reading is meaningless. The value in the flood of these data points rushing at us comes from the patterns within. By the thousands or millions, these data points contain the picture of what is happening and what we can do about it, provided we're creative about connecting the dots and finding the right patterns. And the only way to find these patterns is through creativity and experimentation.

Think about these two factors—creativity and experimentation—and remember how they had so much to do with our efforts in Chapter 3 to set up the data labs, Layered Data Architecture, and other elements of the Agile Data Platform. We spent a lot of that chapter laying the analytics groundwork so we could be agile without inadvertently doing harm through data drift, duplication, and error. Now you see what all this agility is meant for: handling behavioral data!

The more you put agile systems in place, the more people can start thinking about and testing behavioral models and dynamics. Think of how we built the virtual data mart (VDM) so users can have centralized access to data for decentralized use cases. When our users set up a VDM to access production data along with their own data to run specific use cases, what they're doing is looking for patterns in behavioral information. They're experimenting with behavioral data.

All this experimentation is necessary since behavioral processing and thinking are quite different from traditional analytics. We're exploding the volume of data to be considered while simultaneously imposing a big question mark on everything in terms of what may be important. By contrast, transactional data involves fewer data points, and we have a better sense of its importance because most of it is directly linked to a sale or transaction.

Behavioral processing shows us many data points, and many ways to value data. For example, tightly coupled data is the data that's heavily structured and rules-bound. If you were analyzing clickstream data for an e-commerce web site, this would include your definitions of what constitutes a high-value customer, a gold standard metric across your company. Anyone who wanted to change this definition would have to follow a strict process, and those changes would be controlled by a select few.

Meanwhile, loosely coupled data is data that has less structure and fewer contingencies. In the clickstream example, loosely coupled data may include a pairing of a customer ID with a certain session, or a customer ID tagged to a Google search ad campaign or a button on the company's home page. Loosely coupled data can include tens of thousands of tags denoting the kinds of sessions that users had, where they came from, what they clicked on, and so on.

Finally, noncoupled data is the purest, raw form of data. Its usefulness may not even be apparent at first glance, but it could come in handy later. Social media chatter could be one example, as could weather and traffic data.

Bear in mind that your infrastructure must keep up with the capacity demands that come with behavioral processing; and, depending on the use case, those demands may be considerable. The example of money laundering readily comes to mind for Partha Sen. He's founder and CEO of Fuzzy Logix, which specializes in GPU-based and in-database solutions for, among other things, advanced analytics in finance and banking.

"If you look at anti-money-laundering statistics, many organizations are still catching only 20 or 30 percent of perpetrators; and a main concern is volume," he told us. "To legitimize ill-gotten wealth, money laundering can involve several transactions that take time to complete—buying and selling real estate, for instance. If you can only handle a couple of months of data, you miss that life cycle and the patterns may go unnoticed."

"Financial fraud is definitely one of those challenges where finding patterns and signals amid the noise at the scale of big data can be astronomical," said Jacek Becla, Teradata's vice president for technology and innovation. And for Jacek, that analogy is literal: Before joining Teradata in 2017, he served as project manager and head of scalable data systems for the SLAC National Accelerator Laboratory at Stanford University in Menlo Park, California. SLAC conducts cutting-edge research in physics, particle astrophysics, and related disciplines funded by the U.S. Department of Energy (DOE) and the National Science Foundation (NSF). He is also founder of the Extremely Large Database and Data Management (XLDB) community, which hosts annual conferences on challenges related to extreme-scale data sets.

"With astronomy, the scale demands you have distributed data sets, chopping up the sky into chunks of data to analyze. This is where things get complicated, because a typical statistical algorithm grinds to a halt at this scale. It's the same thing with financial fraud and other behavioral data at scale," Jacek explained to us in an interview. "There's no obvious algorithm to detect fraud, the data is not clean, and it's different every time. So it's tricky to build models that you're constantly customizing and validating. You have to think differently and write algorithms that address distributed systems, disk I/O, and related problems that require a lot of customization and adjustments to your models."

BACK INSIDE THE LAYERED DATA ARCHITECTURE

When you understand these complexities, you start to see why it takes robust systems and many kinds of professionals to collaborate around behavioral data at scale. No single employee or team can spot all the ways that a particular form of data may be important, so collaboration is necessary.

Thankfully, we have the Layered Data Architecture in place to render information at multiple levels of complexity for different people to experiment in the contexts they're accustomed to. Sometimes we're in familiar territory, where business users are looking for new instances of patterns and behaviors that have already been established. Other times, we're at square one with a mass of raw data whose patterns remain totally hidden.

Think of a chunk of marble before the sculptor strikes the first blow of the hammer and chisel. The sculptor, in this case, would be the data scientist—indeed, the data artist—working at the lowest and most granular levels of the Layered Data Architecture.

Remember that the Layered Data Architecture is a decomposition framework to get data in its most granular form. This makes it possible for us to examine and reconstitute the data in various levels of complexity for various purposes. While business users may be experimenting in VDMs further up the line, they're doing so on a foundation of research and insight created by data scientists down at Levels 0 and 1, the very lowest layers of the LDA.

These atomic and granular levels, where data sits in its original fidelity, are the seedbed for behavioral data insights. It's where we first start teasing out the signal from the noise. It's a fascinating and challenging realm where highly specialized data scientists take a first look at raw data and try to put it in relation to existing data that we may already have. Here's where we take a first stab at looking for patterns and maybe writing initial algorithms to find more such patterns.

Granularity is key! In previous generations, where capacity was limited and behavioral patterns weren't so important, IT professionals sending data sets to analysts may have thought they were doing everyone a favor by rolling up data—taking minute-by-minute sensor readings and turning them into hourly averages, for example. Today, that's a disservice. Big data platforms can handle the capacity, and every time we roll up, we lose visibility into what's happening.

Granularity reaps value, even if that value is not apparent until later on down the line. We've learned, for instance, that customer sentiment in a call center interaction can be correlated to one very basic factor: duration of the call. People who complain take longer to say it ("My product is the wrong color, plus it took forever to arrive. And then I needed my son to help set it up ..."). People who say they're happy tend to do so succinctly ("Great product. I love it!").

The importance of call duration in this example, however, may initially be hidden amid the noise. In cases like this, where we're first trying to figure out patterns and structures amid the raw data, we find ourselves sifting through some of the most universal and basic pieces of information (date/time stamps or customer identifiers, perhaps) and contending with problems of data quality and consistency (we might find that date/time stamps are logged in several different ways).

A lot of semistructured data modeling takes place at this level. Most of the time, data comes in from business systems and we know what kind of data it is. But we still have to figure out its context and usability. Over time, the goal is to find ways to transcend intent and format of various forms of data. Particularly useful are things like time series, customer identifiers, or some event of interest—whether that happens to be a complaint, threat to leave, compliment, renewal, or something else. You can see how such data wrangling like this can be tough at these early stages. It's a lot like forensics, a mystery to solve by finding commonalities and patterns wherever you can.

REAPING VALUE AND INSIGHT

As we identify more patterns, our confidence level rises. Once we get to the point where business colleagues can help you understand the data and validate it, things start getting familiar ("Ahh, that's a use case around customers not paying their credit card bills. We have to figure out how to get them to pay."). Even then, the analyst may still need to make certain assumptions. It's sort of like being in a play where you have a script, but still need to improvise certain parts.

The good news is that the payoff for this legwork can be tremendous. As we continue to find patterns and make sense across multiple varieties and channels of data, we can begin to harmonize them. Multiple channels or touch points of customer interaction, for instance, can be harmonized into one mega channel, such as an integrated contact history (ICH) file. You can then search for more complex patterns associated with positive or negative customer outcomes.

Assume for a moment you're doing this kind of customer relationship management (CRM) work for a wireless service provider. People are upset with the service, and some are switching providers. We've harmonized three channels: call center notes, trips to a store, and clickstream logs from their web experience. Who went online first? Who went to the store first? Who called the contact center first? In this example, there's a good chance we can examine the sequence of interactions and see how they relate to positive or negative outcomes. Now we have better insight into how and where to prioritize our efforts at customer retention.

How much insight is too much insight? You've probably heard the quote "Just because we can doesn't mean we should." That is certainly something to consider as we realize how fully behavioral data lets us understand our customers. Much of the issue has to do with data privacy. In our experience, customers don't mind if you get to know their preferences and habits per se. But things get creepy if you start indiscriminately sharing those nuances of their life with other companies.

Behavioral knowledge and data privacy need to go hand in hand: we like to say companies should be customized without being creepy. It's almost like your customer has entered into a contract or covenant with you: "I'm going to let you know about me so you can make my customer experience easy and seamless; but I don't want you to sell or leak that knowledge to everyone else."

PROACTIVE DATA STANDARDS AND DESIGNING FOR THE UNKNOWN

You probably noticed that we've made more than one reference in this chapter to artistic realms like sculpture and live theater productions. These references are intentional: the data scientist looking for patterns amid all the noise is blending mathematical and engineering expertise with no small amount of artistry in making innovative assumptions and coming up with novel theories and insights.

That creative guesswork can be time-consuming, however, and a certain amount can be avoided if we do a better job standardizing the way we collect and use data to begin with. We need to record and manage data with an eye toward how it's going to be analyzed in the future, even if we don't know exactly what that future will look like.

We need, in other words, to design for the unknown. The roll-ups and optimizations we talked about earlier in this chapter may work okay for today's known applications, but our analytic architecture and design choices today should not inhibit new and currently unknown use cases tomorrow.

For example, technologists often place clickstream data into session containers on file systems to make things like bot detection or per-visit analysis easy. But doing so sacrifices entirely different use cases—situations that may not start with individual website visits such as financial checkouts, call center interactions, or machine/sensor events.

Whenever we place data in a certain order, grouping, or structure to allow for one type of access today, chances are that we may complicate things tomorrow as patterns and questions shift. That's bad news, because we cannot afford to redesign or rearchitect the data over and over. Yet, this is what's most likely happening right now in your company over and over.

If we remedy such issues—standardizing wherever possible, avoiding roll-ups, and preserving the granular detail when staging data for analysis—we reduce friction, enhance governance, and make our organization better and faster at wrangling data. Few companies today do this really well, meaning anybody who is diligent about standardization can get real competitive advantage.

Dell is one such company. In Chapter 3, we heard from Vice President Jennifer Felch about Dell's evolution toward global manufacturing processes and infrastructure. To its credit, the Dell analytics team understood clearly and early the value of standardization. "When we organized the company into some globally shared capabilities, that's where we had this realization that there were different processes, and even different definitions, of key data pieces," she told us.

"We had regional general managers, regional manufacturing, and regional IT systems," she said. "When it came time to set up a global manufacturing site, we had to ask, 'Are we going to support three or four different inputs and processes, or are we going to standardize before we go? Do we spend three times the integration costs, or do we just do it right from the start?' And so we decided to standardize from the very beginning."

We've spent the past few pages looking over the shoulders of experts who first examine our data for patterns and context. But not everyone is a data scientist, and we need to make sure analytics is accessible more broadly across the organization. The Sentient Enterprise, after all, is about creating a world where all people in the company work together to prioritize corporate information and execute analytics. That's where the Collaborative Ideation Platform—Stage 3 of the Sentient Enterprise journey—comes in.

CHAPTER 5

The Collaborative Ideation Platform

W e're now well on our way in the Sentient Enterprise journey to maturing analytics at scale as we grow our businesses. In Stage 1, we built the foundation for managing data by creating the Agile Data Platform. In Stage 2, we introduced the Behavioral Data Platform to harness that added dimension of possibilities within the vast world of human- and sensor-driven behavioral data. Despite having these agile systems and the capacity in place to support such a rich analytics environment, however, we're still left with a lot of complexities that can stymie progress.

Remember that a chief mandate is not just to engage a broad range of users in analytics, but to ensure that they can work and innovate together. Too much data and too many insights that aren't coordinated or vetted for value can quickly become barriers to this collaboration. The only way to survive as we scale our businesses is to foster an analytics environment where a lot of different people can collaborate and share ideas. It's no secret, then, that we chose the "Collaborative Ideation Platform" as our name for Stage 3 of the Sentient Enterprise journey.

This chapter deals with how to set up this Collaborative Ideation Platform for agile, intuitive, and crowdsourced cooperation throughout the organization in ways that remain simple and intuitive, even at scale. We'll learn how to leverage the LinkedIn- and Facebook-style social media conventions we previewed in Chapter 2 to help the organization understand which ideas, projects, and people get followed, liked, shared, and so on. In the process, we'll see how these new and fast ways to connect humans and data are outperforming traditional analytic approaches—including centralized metadata management—that tend to break down and become nearly impossible to maintain at scale.

AVOIDING "ANTI-SOCIAL" ANALYTICS

The truth is that all the analytic heft and agile systems in the world won't do much good if our users are still going it alone, following hunches in uncoordinated ways and—if they're not ignoring metadata altogether—relying on a few people they know for a piecemeal approach to metadata. How do we recognize value, share context,

FIVE STAGES

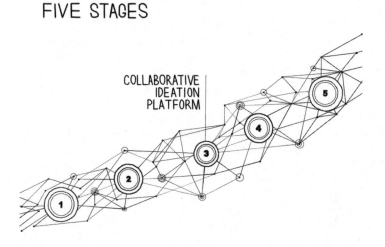

COLLABORATIVE
IDEATION
PLATFORM

and socialize best practices along with lessons learned throughout the company? How do we ensure quality control and knowledge transfer between data scientists and users, in order to stay on the right track as we give analytic freedom to everyone?

In short, how do we avoid the mistake of preserving the same old company silos on top of the expensive and powerful new analytics platforms we just built? Even if we reach the point of getting folks familiar with virtual data marts (VDMs), the sandboxes for user experiments around data that we talked about in Chapter 3, how do we connect these various individual uses cases in our larger analytics efforts?

If the dynamic and exciting LinkedIn for Analytics environment mentioned in Chapter 2 is sounding like a good solution right now, then you're right on the money! That's because LinkedIn for Analytics is a core feature of the Collaborative Ideation Platform.

The LinkedIn for Analytics approach is designed to solve several problems at once. We need to keep business users from getting stuck in avoidance mode when it comes to interacting with IT staff, and these challenges include psychology and organizational culture as well as technology. Social media conventions help chart both what we actually do with data and how we talk about it. Users feel engaged, and we reap insights through the patterns we see around the ideas, projects, and people that get followed, shared, or linked.

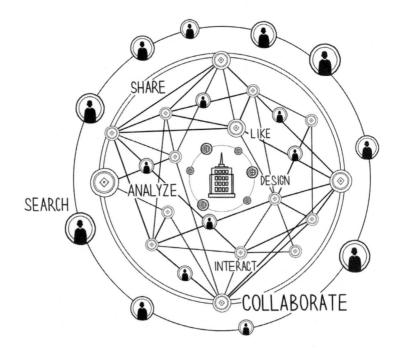

To these social networking strategies, we add incentives like gamification—where we hold contests for the right answer and/or give special recognition for success—to make analytics more approachable and even fun. This helps expand our circle of engagement, and this participation generates the kind of experimentation and contextual understanding that brings information to life and fully leverages it for value and competitive advantage.

THE PROBLEM OF METADATA AT SCALE

When done correctly, our crowdsourced and socialized approach to analytic insight happens to solve one of the biggest problems of scale that companies face as they grow larger. We're talking about the management of metadata, that all-important data about data that acts as a card catalog for the digital age, boosting value and usefulness of original data and files by describing the contents and context of that information.

The problem is that centralized metadata invariably breaks down at scale. That's because centralized metadata traditionally relies on human analysts, and humans don't scale. Whenever we create more complexity—involving not just the volume of data, but also the variety and velocity—analysts tend to lose control over the flood of algorithms, visualizations, dashboards, and tables coming at them.

Consider the example of clickstream data. Look at the average e-commerce site and you will see lots of drop-down menus, tables, product recommendations, user reviews, promotional deals, customer or purchase details, and other information. In order to capture what people are doing, we put tags on all these visual and navigational elements (as far back as 2010, for example, eBay already had more than 60,000 unique tags on its website).

Even if we have the technology to capture all this information, there's just no way for humans to keep track of what's important. To stick with our example of clickstreams, our own experience is that anything above 100 tags is too much for people to keep track of. Metadata is through the roof, and trying to manage it in traditional, IT-centric ways has become a recurring nightmare for many businesses.

Indeed, most metadata collection and management projects today are pretty ugly and time-consuming ordeals, led by IT and stigmatized by everyone else as burdensome, slow, and document-intensive processes. Somehow, this sad state of affairs has endured as the norm. Before we developed the LinkedIn for Analytics approach, in fact, we had never heard of a single case of a large-scale metadata project driven by business users as a community of shared interests and needs.

IT staff at companies today are constantly having to sell the value of metadata to colleagues. But since IT is leading the effort, the methods aren't very user friendly or state of the art, making it even harder to get business users to see the point.

In attracting collaboration, you'll find the carrot is always more useful than the stick. As we'll see in our discussion of adoption toward the end of this chapter, the more we can leverage convenience and modern design patterns and websites that attract traffic, the less we need to lean on rules and corporate mandates that enforce their usage. Furthermore, we need to designate personnel to serve as counselors and moderators to facilitate and support this approach. These internal evangelists, coupled with internal marketing and public relations (PR), are terribly important in order to foster these new collaborative communities.

Why must we pay attention to these details? Because if we don't, people simply resort to the same work-arounds and fiefdoms they always have: They pick up the phone, walk down the hall, or send an e-mail to a colleague to get an answer. They keep a lot of Excel spreadsheets—more like cheat sheets—in a bid to avoid the slow, cumbersome, and expensive metadata processes led by IT.

COLLABORATION AND CONTEXT AT SCALE

If you have a fairly small operation, you may be able to survive with a traditional approach like having your centralized team of analysts assign metadata so the rest of the company knows what information is important and where to find it. But in large organizations dealing with big data today, that traditional approach can quickly break down. As we've said, humans don't scale the way data does, and a corps of a hundred or even a thousand analysts still won't be able to keep up with the job of documenting the huge volumes of information and lightning-fast data streams coming at them.

That's why we need to turn to the wisdom of the crowd: specifically, the hundreds or thousands of people within your organization who work with data. At its core, the Collaborative Ideation Platform is a combination of LinkedIn for Analytics plus an analytics on analytics (AonA) team that charts everyone's interactions and insights to learn what data is most relevant and useful to the enterprise. (We'll talk in more detail about the AonA component of the Collaborative Ideation Platform a little later in this chapter.)

This process of letting people collaborate on data freely, with checks and balances from hard-core analysts, creates a system where data's value and context become naturally clear, without the hassle of costly and time-consuming documentation safaris that IT leads and everyone else in the company runs away from.

The Collaborative Ideation Platform we're building in this chapter leverages analytical models to examine what your community of data scientists and other analysts is doing with data, but we're not simply interested in their specific queries or dashboard activity. We want to provide a forum to capture and analyze commentary and discussion among these folks, complete with social media conventions to let people "like" a certain analytic approach, "follow" a particular analyst, or monitor data sets that are popular and trending.

Some companies have gone in this direction already, including eBay, whose DataHub we discussed in Chapter 2. Over time, DataHub evolved from a simple social website into what is now a fully analytics-based social platform capable of ingesting query logs of all known analytical systems in order to share, recommend, and highlight what individuals and teams are doing with analytics throughout the organization.

In addition, Gerhard Kress, vice president of mobility data services at Siemens, whom we first met in Chapter 2, says his company has embraced its own version of a Collaborative Ideation Platform for both internal and external partners working together on Siemens Mobility's rail systems:

"We have the same data foundation for service people out in the field, all the way up to the engineers who created the locomotives, to jointly look at customer issues and how we can address them by having everybody share the same truths and everybody having access to the same information from the field. We have a similar platform with some of our customers. We provide data from sensors and diagnostic procedures on the train. It's their asset, so it's their data, and this platform allows us to collaborate. From our end we can add engineering understanding to clarify insights and help the customers understand what these insights mean for them. From their end, customers provide information on how they run their operations, how they're planning their timetables, and what they might need from us to be more successful. Together, we're jointly creating something that's much bigger than what any of us could do on our own."

Regardless of your exact approach, the goal is to keep people engaged and invested in data to efficiently harvest the insights so that your understanding of data can scale along with your growing data volumes and business operations.

MERCHANDISING ANALYTIC INSIGHTS

How exactly do we guide the user community and capture insights in these seamless ways we've been talking about? The key is to not just socialize data among business users, but to merchandise it!

Think of how we shop on Amazon or eBay. We search, we promote, we recommend, we follow. Over time, the analytics running underneath that online experience learn what's important or relevant to us; those insights are then used to tailor searches and increase the relevance of the recommendations and product suggestions we see.

In the Collaborative Ideation Platform, we're essentially doing the same thing with data and analytics; we're applying the same form of merchandising to the analytics network within an enterprise—promoting and recommending questions, people, and answers that an employee might be interested in based on previous queries and activity.

Here's an example: Imagine that one of your business analysts is working on a project. He types out a query, perhaps a question like "Who are all the repeat customers who are male?" The system then translates his query into SQL language that will pull the data he needs. It also makes auto-complete suggestions based on similar queries other users may have asked before.

Next, the system recommends other people in the company working on similar projects, just like LinkedIn and Facebook might recommend friends to you, or Amazon might recommend products for you based on what you've previously bought or searched for. Perhaps you're not even sure what questions to ask of the database and you need to tap into human knowledge first. The Collaborative Ideation Platform includes ways to ask for help, similar to Quora or StackExchange. This creates a community within your organization where employees ask for advice and learn from one another.

Questions can also get voted up or down, so the top concerns and problems facing the business become readily apparent. To enable deeper investigation, employees can create longer posts and articles, with charts and visualizations to explain their ideas. This provides a forum for storytelling around data, where analysts can describe the steps they took to arrive at a conclusion and share their innovative ideas.

Remember from Chapter 3 how our Stage 1 Agile Data Platform allows us to log everything and even replay all those steps someone took during the experimentation process to look for clues and pivot points to value. Now in Stage 3, that functionality enables a recommended data set or analysis to even come with visualizations by people who had worked on similar problems in the past.

The Collaborative Ideation Platform puts all users on the same playing field and invites them to come to the table, no matter what their areas of expertise. It brings multiple experiences and perspectives together as the system helps analysts learn from one another, dig deeper into complex business challenges, and refine previous solutions. This also makes it easier to train new employees in their first weeks as they get up to speed on the most important recent discoveries they'll need to know about and follow.

STAYING ON THE PATH TO VALUE THROUGH ANALYTICS ON ANALYTICS

What about incorrect answers? What about groupthink and everyone getting on the bandwagon for a certain algorithm or approach that may be more popular than it is useful? Let's be clear: The Collaborative Ideation Platform does not eliminate these problems—it's entirely possible to collaborate on ideas that are wrongheaded. But the platform we're building gives us several ways to more easily identify and correct problems when they do occur.

First, there's the built-in transparency that comes with connecting your entire corps of analytics professionals in a LinkedIn for Analytics environment. The chances go up that somebody will notice a flawed approach and/or suggest another way of doing things when we socialize the entire company together. We're no longer in a patchwork environment of information silos where people stick to their own fiefdoms of favored coworkers to collaborate with. We're now in a wide-open network for information sharing that tends to be self-correcting.

Think of Wikipedia and the collaborative editing that happens among that online encyclopedia's vast community (more than 26 million users of the English language site alone). Research shows that the perpetual crowdsourcing effort to correct errors has put Wikipedia's accuracy above the 99 percent mark—on a par with the *Encyclopaedia Britannica* and other respected reference publications.

We've got a similar process of self-correction among users happening within our recommended LinkedIn for Analytics environment. But an even more powerful force for accuracy and value is the AonA function we've set up to listen to business users and interpret everything that happens among them.

We mentioned earlier in this chapter how the Collaborative Ideation Platform is a combination of the LinkedIn for Analytics environment plus the AonA team of data scientists who model, cluster, and analyze what people are doing. The simple fact is that you can't have LinkedIn for Analytics without also having that dedicated AonA team whose only job is to examine everyone's interactions to learn what data is most relevant and useful to the enterprise. In a sense, you can think of AonA as your internal equivalent of clickstream, sensor data, call center events, or customer service logs.

Remember how we looked in on the data scientists in Chapter 4 as they worked at the granular levels of the Layered Data Architecture to interpret patterns and value from outside data sources? Our AonA team—usually three to five people—is doing the same thing with the data generated inside the company from users in our LinkedIn for Analytics community. The team is essentially creating its own Layered Data Architecture dedicated to this one focus area of our internal business user community.

Our AonA team's job is to record and analyze all activity and all search results. With this information they write algorithms to optimize search or highlight related projects. Think back to what we said earlier in this chapter about the merchandising of analytic insights, and you now see how this is the team that's responsible for the recommendations and auto-complete search functions that help everyone connect with the most relevant people, projects, and data in the company.

When someone may be going down the wrong path, AonA can identify this and help correct the course by putting rules on top of user behavior, based on outcomes and lessons learned from previous user activity. It's a seamless and hassle-free way to slide in best practices that involves more than just algorithms. We're looking at the context of what other people have asked, plus what the data science and analytics teams can tell us about where these questions have taken us in the past in terms of relevance, applicability, or value.

Agility, self-service, and collaboration require AonA. As an analytical competitor who is pushing the limits of data and insights, you cannot leave the evolution of these capabilities up to chance. This is especially true given that you are ingesting large amounts of platform and processing data into self-service collaboration environments.

Remember that 30 to 50 percent of your processing may ultimately get devoted to these open platforms, so your operational excellence requires you to know what is efficient and effective—and what is not. This understanding should ideally extend to the user community, with activity-based costing that creates a feedback loop so every participant of the analytical ecosystem knows how many resources a project is consuming and what it costs the company to do so.

ADOPTION TAKES TIME

In a perfect world, it'd be great to see every person in the company working in the Collaborative Ideation Platform right away. But the Sentient Enterprise deals with the real world. You can't just flip a switch, send a company-wide memo, and have everyone on board the next day.

As we discussed in our Introduction and Chapter 1, the Sentient Enterprise proposes a very different way of doing analytics that involves both procedural and cultural transitions that can't happen overnight. That's why we recommend you introduce the Collaborative Ideation Platform in the same manner that we introduce other pieces of the Sentient Enterprise puzzle: start small and operate almost as if you're a start-up within your own company.

You can take the best social software on the planet, drop it into the whole company, and see it die if you don't nurture it the right way. There's no way to launch something like this and get it magically adopted. You instead need to build small teams that promote and mentor this environment. These are the early adopters—a select group of, say, 20 or 30 people who take part in a pilot effort.

Don't advertise or oversell what you're doing to the whole company; in the early stages, just stick with your core group of interested people using the system. Focus on a few early wins and success stories that will then inspire more adopters. Maybe you're up to 50 people on board after the first two months, and then more people join as time and success stories continue.

What about the holdouts? Just as with Facebook, LinkedIn, and the other social platforms we're emulating, you'll find folks who just don't want to sign up. Our message is: don't force things. There will always be people who won't want to be on the grid. You may have 50 to 70 percent of people not wanting to participate, but that's not a success criterion. Your barometer for success has more to do with what's being accomplished by that sliver of your workforce that has gone ahead and adopted the Collaborative Ideation Platform.

Getting just three or four percent of users to adopt could take weeks or months, but this level of activity can still reap some great use cases. Even in a large company, 50 or 100 people can make a huge difference. As you build more capabilities, keep directing more and more people there.

Doing a company-wide launch with no good content or success stories is guaranteed to fail. Instead, pick those initial users, educate them, and help them be successful. You may even get to the point of hosting your own internal data conferences within the company. These are the steps that ultimately let success speak for itself.

Trust that this ramp-up piloting approach will work, because it has for companies like Siemens. "We carve out a certain area, take a limited investment, and bring people in to drive home a specific issue that will really bring value to the organization," Gerhard Kress told us.

"We give them a task with data and have them come back in a few months with a result. That's the only entry," he explained. "From there, you can scale it up. Bring more people in and increase the reach of your solution through the whole enterprise. Otherwise, I don't believe it's possible."

OPERATIONALIZING INSIGHTS

You've created the Collaborative Ideation Platform to smash hierarchies and have all people in an organization work with each other, not against each other. As a result, you're now getting thousands of ideas and viable insights a day. That's great! But now you need to do something about those ideas and insights.

From understanding to doing is a big step, and it's one that most companies stumble over. Sadly, however, there are still companies out there today where the only way these visualizations reach the C-suite is in the form of artwork on the walls. Buttonhole a senior executive to ask what's actually being done as a result of that picture on the wall and you may not get much of an answer.

All too often, we marvel at the insights that analytics bring to the table, but we don't take the next steps of acting on those insights to drive change. The decision to do so gets lost at the executive level, and that's something we're going to fix in the next stage of the Sentient Enterprise journey: the Analytical Application Platform.

CHAPTER **6**

The Analytical Application Platform

Our work so far has built what you might think of as a company-wide innovation funnel, with the capacity to manage floods of behavioral data and simplify collaboration, governance, and metadata at scale. But especially in large organizations that may have hundreds, or even thousands, of people with "analyst" in their job titles, we need to make sure this broad user community has the right tools to actually do something with all the insights being generated by data. We need, in other words, to turn insights into action.

"There will always be high-end data science issues, but most business problems can be solved by the business users," said General Motors chief data officer A. Charles Thomas. "Those business managers need to understand the levers to pull, but not necessarily know all the engineering that goes into the analytics."

"If you want people to stop submitting tickets and get them to start thinking more analytically on their own, you have to package up the complexity into accessible tools," Charles told us in an interview. "That's essentially what we've done here. We're giving them the means to follow that spark of curiosity that might get them saying, 'Hmm, there's a spike over here . . . an aberration over there. . . . Let's experiment a little to figure out why.'"

FIVE STAGES

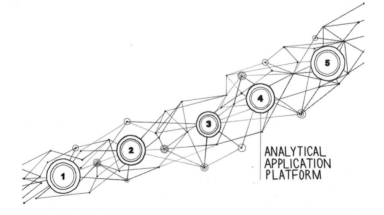

ANALYTICAL
APPLICATION
PLATFORM

TURNING ANALYTIC INSIGHT INTO ACTION ACROSS THE ORGANIZATION

That "spark of curiosity," as Charles aptly calls it, is perhaps one of the most valuable assets in the workforce, an asset that grows as we share data broadly across the organization. We're far enough along in our journey to recognize that if you keep access to data centralized, you're also keeping the capacity for innovation centralized—and limited. At the same time, simply opening up the data floodgates to your workforce, without a solid strategy, will create more confusion than success. That's why creating the Analytical Application Platform is so crucial as a self-service, on-demand environment for users to follow their hunches and turn insights into action.

"I certainly believe the CDO's charter involves democratizing data and giving everyday business users as much power as we can. And when we hand over a tool, that's what's happening; we're helping them get as smart and as independent as possible." explained Charles. "Sometimes there's a bit of what I call 'pushing them out of the nest' and getting them to realize that, with the right tools, they can solve some of the easier analytics problems on their own, not write so many tickets, and, when they do ask for help, it's for the tougher questions that you really need deeper data science to answer."

When we build analytical apps, we're expanding the company's seedbed for analytic insight and value. However, just as we shouldn't simply open up the data floodgates to the entire company without a framework like analytical apps, neither should we simply crank out analytical apps without some support systems in place. "While it's important to keep bureaucracy to a minimum, analytical apps do need to operate within a certain organizational framework," Charles told us in our interview. He went on to describe what he calls a company-wide system for "insight governance":

"At the highest levels, we have an Analytics Leadership Council—sort of like the 'heads of state' in analytics for each line of business. That's about 15 or so people who meet monthly, or as needed, to talk about problems, priorities, talent, recruiting, and best practices. It's very methodical and tied to outcomes like driving revenue, delighting customers, mitigating risk, leveraging metrics, and so on. App development is one of the things on the agenda, and we have relationship managers to gauge analytics needs within the organization and coordinate quick development of the apps. Plus, there's a community of super-users within the various company divisions to answer some of the intermediate questions. Advanced data scientists are always available to help when roadblocks or deeper analytic challenges arise. But the beauty of the system is the workload for these experts is naturally skewed toward these tougher challenges, where they're needed most!"

Charles also explained how this coordinated approach for insight governance remains agile and adaptable to many different departments and business problems:

"My job is to find the broadest possible landscape where data can help inform business decisions. With any organization, you'll find that some departments and job functions may be more receptive than others. Mobile and online divisions tend to be familiar already with the value of data, for instance, and marketing departments might already know how you can help them with specific campaigns that have clear measures of success. You might need to talk through things a bit more with places like an HR, legal, or physical asset management department. But even in these areas, the value of analytics becomes clear once you demonstrate, for example, how a digital analysis of legal language can reveal suggested changes that might make things better for your customer. And because we're such a large company, even small changes in something like that can have a big impact. That's why I ultimately consider the chief data officer's charter to be anywhere we can inform business decisions at scale."

When designed and implemented correctly, analytical applications and the insight governance framework that supports them can put data insights to work for the organization, even in the face of tough and demanding business challenges like the CRM headwinds Charles and his colleagues at Wells Fargo successfully navigated in Chapter 4. In fact, that's when analytics can really shine by helping what we've come to refer to as "lighthouse customers"—internal partners who are struggling with a tough challenge—to create solutions and ultimately showcase for the rest of the company the value of agile analytics.

"The best time to talk through digital improvements is when you're having challenges and issues," Charles summarized toward the end of our interview. "Whenever someone says, 'Let's take a step back and make sure we're doing right by our customers,' I say, 'While you're doing that, let's make sure we automate what we can and make things easier and more efficient.'"

LESSONS FROM THE CLOUD

Wells Fargo and some of the other leading-edge companies we've discussed in this book are still more the exception than the rule. Many organizations continue to exist in traditional data warehouse environments that are lacking on the action side, and this isn't really isolated to any particular vendor or proprietary approach. Indeed, take a look at most any traditional business intelligence (BI) tool or dashboard, and you're often left with a sense of "Now what?"

The reason for this is we're still trying to innovate by painstakingly inventing and reinventing work flows and applications. That's what we're going to fix in this chapter. Fortunately, we have a solid point of reference as we set about making improvements: in building the Analytical Application Platform, it's useful to see how cloud computing has paved the way to operationalize analytics quickly and at scale.

In the old days, if you had only a few servers to deal with, you could stick to a customized plan to build your capacity and analytics; there's not really the need for automation and repeatability in order to program and manage such a limited amount of resources. But the cloud has changed everything.

In the cloud, we have exponential provisioning of computer resources in minutes, instead of the weeks or months you'd have to wait to provision the same capacity in a typical IT shop. This drastic reduction in provisioning time frames enables work to happen and scale up much more quickly. The problem is that things are scaling so quickly that no amount of human support can keep pace.

That's why business success in the cloud requires a wholesale rethinking of work flow and governance. Those who've excelled in the cloud have learned to take an app approach, combining fast IT provisioning with agile and repeatable frameworks that allow all this compute capability to roll out into mainline business processes.

Without such frameworks, agility gets stuck at the halfway mark: you've made a portion of your infrastructure and internal IT processes more agile, but you may not have actually made a difference for your company by building fast and repeatable paths to action for your business users. The takeaway is clear for those of us building the Sentient Enterprise: we need to complete the agility picture with platforms and systems that let us develop an analytics solution that lots of people can use right away and at scale.

Right away and at scale. Consider those priorities for a moment: They're probably the cloud's top two selling points; they also happen to explain the essence of apps and why Stage 4 is all about building an app-centric platform. Apps are the perfect way to do things right away and at scale. Just ask Robert Nay, the teenager we told you about in Chapter 1 who used an app development platform to quickly create his Bubble Ball game and get it downloaded 400,000 times in its first day of release.

CREATING AN APP ECONOMY FOR THE ENTERPRISE

Robert Nay and other young boys and girls can build their own mobile apps on a Facebook API or use Apple Watch SDK data without having to understand all the complexities of that data. Nor do they have to think too much about the finer details of governance and provisioning when they send cool new games viral to hundreds of thousands of users.

What if your business provided this kind of app framework to enable analytics follow-through in your own organization? For all the reasons we've just explained, an app-centric platform is the way to achieve the kind of seamless and iterative functionality we need at scale.

Our mandate, then, is to bring an app-style economy from the consumer world into the enterprise. This gets us beyond today's reality, where only a handful of IT people write code. We need to reach the point where we have zero-cost deployment, like in the app store, without creating added stress for IT.

Just as with consumer apps, we must embed complexities, simplify the development process, create data engines that "just work," and promote ease of use and accessibility. Once embedded in an app tool created by a developer or two, these easy and accessible analytic processes can be used again and again by thousands of colleagues.

As an example, let's say the enterprise needs to calculate the lifetime value of a customer. An Analytical Application Platform allows a developer or a two-person team to write as little as 50 lines of code to start a new customer satisfaction index. This may involve advanced analytical capabilities—like new clustering, graphing, and n-dimensional pathing—to greatly reduce the amount of subsequent coding required to generate analytical outcomes.

In this context, it's important to note how new technologies are making an impact, but often in different ways than advertised. The vast majority of business users, analysts, and even some of your data scientists will never dive that deeply into the lowest levels of at-scale programming. Instead, they'll need these capabilities delivered for them as an app. Remember that your ultimate app should be accessible to the business users; and today's users demand languages like Python or advanced forms of SQL to describe and codify their analytical needs.

Once the app is created, you can have countless other teams—including those with limited coding knowledge—download the app from an app ecosystem or store within the company and use it in their own reporting. In this scenario, you have an embedded and repeatable process; and you suddenly have a lot more doers in your corporate culture.

An added beauty here is that the value of these applications grows exponentially as people use the platform. As more and more people engage in the Analytical Application Platform, we start to gather more context for who's using which apps, who is making progress, and who else is following that progress. We're now looking at a rich ecosystem where a lot more tagging and behavioral information is generated around the apps. This, in turn, fuels better analytics and applications.

Right about now, you may be getting a bit of déjà vu and thinking of the Collaborative Ideation Platform. That's because that same process of socializing data in that LinkedIn for Analytics environment is happening here as well. The difference is that we're generating even more value for the enterprise because we're now applying the data socialization capabilities of the Collaborative Ideation Platform to the sophisticated but accessible performance work flows represented by our growing universe of analytic apps.

Our Analytical Application Platform, in other words, is governed by the same social-media-style dynamics we put in place when building the Collaborative Ideation Platform: people can find apps, like apps, follow apps, and merchandize them just as we explained how to merchandize individual sets of data in Chapter 5. But we're now merchandizing something more than just the value of data. By merchandizing apps, we're all of the sudden merchandizing performance and prebuilt work flows that may involve a combination of multiple technologies. We are merchandizing action!

The analytics on analytics (AonA) functionality we saw in the Collaborative Ideation Platform applies in Stage 4 as well. Here, we establish a feedback loop to understand who's using which apps, and how effectively. Whenever a new app is released, how many people are using it? How efficient does it seem to be? Where and how should we tweak or correct course? Throughout, we put a premium on keeping this AonA governance seamless and relatively hassle-free, since our governance team must support the Analytical Application Platform without slowing things down for the user community.

DEVOPS TO MAKE IT REAL

Throughout this book, we've tried to describe our journey at a depth that most business users will be able to follow. But, as with our Layered Data Architecture discussion in Chapter 3 and some of the implementation tips we share in Chapter 8, now is one of those times when we must provide a certain amount of technical context to make things real and concrete for IT managers and developers looking to implement the Sentient Enterprise vision.

Stage 4 is about literally setting up the Analytical Application Platform on top of the Collaborative Ideation Platform: Our own, enterprise-specific app store lives there. We can package up work flows and make them reusable, sharable, and repeatable, and all the social media and AonA conventions apply. By building Stage 4, we're now applying an agility framework not just to data and insights, but to performance itself.

One development approach that's particularly relevant here in Stage 4 is something that's called DevOps. The term is a mashup of development and operations, and DevOps is a way to boost agility by bringing these two worlds more closely together. When you improve collaboration between developers and IT operations teams, you invariably get better quality assurance, faster delivery of software, lower failure rates for new releases, and quicker software updates stemming from user requests.

The DevOps approach relies on more open communication and information sharing between developers and IT operations people throughout the delivery pipeline for new applications. A lot of emphasis is placed on ensuring this open communication and automating and standardizing simple processes wherever possible. Some have described the crux of DevOps as promoting "empathy" as the whole organization adopts a more common and application-centric understanding of IT development. For the purposes of our discussion, the DevOps dynamics we're most concerned with are repeatability, version control, and security.

Repeatability is essentially about not having to reinvent the wheel every time you're looking to deploy or update an analytics technique throughout the company. It's about not having to keep track of every incremental change or tweak that your data analyst community makes to work flow or projects. This kind of seamless version control is a cornerstone of repeatability, and it needs to be intuitive and hassle-free.

The beauty of combining DevOps with an app-centric environment is that an app platform can slide in repeatability and version control underneath the developer and anyone else in the company without them needing to read or know about it. It's just one more process that's embedded into the app. Remember that we talked about seamless governance in Chapter 5? It's the same idea here.

As a simple analogy, imagine the difference between writing in Microsoft Word versus composing in Google Docs. If you draft a complicated document with multiple authors and reviewers via MS Word, you'll likely encounter a flood of back-and-forth e-mails, with many versions. Some poor soul in the organization will need to spend half a day reconciling all the changes that may be happening concurrently by—but completely off the respective radars of—multiple users.

Google Docs, by contrast, allows multiple users to collaborate around a single document in ways that capture and archive changes automatically and seamlessly. If you need to go back and look at the history, you can; but it's not forced upon you as a roadblock to agility. This book, for instance, was composed via Google Docs, a godsend when you consider we've got two authors and multiple researchers, fact checkers, proofreaders, and publishing executives all convening around the same text.

More to the point, think of GitHub. Upwards of 11 million people use GitHub to discover and contribute to more than 28 million projects. Thanks to GitHub repositories and other intuitive tools, all these folks can experiment while the system holds all the past versions of everyone's code, as well as the current ones. Otherwise there'd be chaos and anarchy. You can see how these principles of repeatability and version control are crucial to any analytics application platform at a large company trying to innovate and produce at scale.

Things are very much the same when it comes to security. It is easier to build security and access protocols into an app. It's a question of programming it once and letting those parameters do the work day in and day out as people use the app. Only people allowed to see the data are allowed to see the app. Sometimes, you need to make adjustments to your security parameters; and a seamless version control allows those changes to be logged and remain traceable. Accountability is never lost, since you always have a clear trail of data and attributes.

Again, we can thank the cloud for forcing us to think in terms of DevOps and app-centric platforms for the enterprise. We've always stood to benefit from these methods. The difference is that we're now operating at such a scale and iterating on so many servers and elements that we absolutely need them!

LESS ETL . . .

Especially as we enter the home stretch of our five-stage journey toward sentience, it's important to take a slightly deeper dive at this point to understand just what's happening with our data. As we continue to build the Analytical Application Platform and lay the groundwork for truly agile and autonomous analytics, we're now faced with the need to fundamentally rethink how we access and define data.

The essential function of data in modern architectures is morphing from the traditional, after-the-fact pulling and defining of data to a more proactive stance that involves platforms to actively monitor (or, as we'll learn shortly, "listen" to) data as it comes in. As this happens, we're increasingly moving away from the once-ubiquitous practice of extracting, transforming, and loading (ETL) data.

Let's be clear: ETL is not necessarily a bad or unneeded thing. The process of extracting, or reading, data from a database; transforming it in ways that it can be placed into another database; and then loading, or writing, data to that target database has been a mainstay of analytics for decades. That means, to some extent, we need to accept the ongoing presence of some legacy systems and the ETL-related staffing, software licensing, and hardware that go along with managing those systems.

As we stress in our Introduction and in several of Chapter 8's implementation tips, the Sentient Enterprise is a realistic and long-term journey that—especially for large businesses with legacy systems—requires multiple generations of analytics architectures to coexist as we slowly evolve the company to a more autonomous analytics posture. So, for the foreseeable future, we'll see an ongoing role for ETL. We should also note that ETL tools have evolved somewhat in the face of big data to make the process quicker, cheaper, and more user-friendly.

That said, even the most recent ETL improvements, including data replication functions, change data capture, and other value adds, will never be good enough because they're all based on an increasingly obsolete worldview of data. It's not that the software is bad. It's that the whole approach to ETL is limited by the fact that we're reverse engineering data integration to begin with.

"The mapping of data to its real-world meaning—that's the most fundamental piece for any decision making process," observed Dell's Jennifer Felch. "If we don't have a common understanding of what it means in the real world, then you can't scale and you can't take action."

Nonetheless, even today, you'll see engineers building a new manufacturing line, website, billing system, or some other asset without giving much thought up front about data integration. That's because they're used to sending ETL teams in after the fact to go find and integrate that data. The problem is that those teams are not experts in that manufacturing line, website, or billing system. They're usually business intelligence folks who've been trained on an ETL tool.

The fact is that many companies today still have significant investment in people, skills, software, and hardware to do nothing but ETL. But the teams that do this aren't totally familiar with the subject matter of the data. That produces fewer insights and more errors. Furthermore, the reliance on human teams makes ETL vulnerable to the same death knell we first sounded on centralized metadata in Chapter 2: like centralized metadata, ETL relies on centralized human teams that often become the bottlenecks, because humans don't scale the way data does.

We clearly need a better way to understand data and its meanings, especially if we hope to enable autonomous decisioning at scale in our upcoming Stage 5.

. . . MORE "DATA LISTENING"

Traditionally, you have IT systems adopting an ETL-driven waterfall model: When there's a new feature or app, people make a formal request for data. It's always after the fact that people grab and analyze the data. So why don't we instead let the engineers who are building systems integrate the data to begin with? Why shouldn't engineers building an app ask, up front, "What kind of data does this new app I'm working on generate?"

Imagine how many more insights you could gather, the human errors you could prevent, and the people-hours you could save if you didn't have to hire a team of specialists to build an ETL system. Imagine if you could instead listen to data as it arrives, instead of always operating under the old, ETL-driven pull model of reverse engineering data's usefulness. Fortunately, we do just that in Stage 4 by developing capabilities for "enterprise listening" to support our Analytical Application Platform.

We've shared in the course of this book many Sentient Enterprise building blocks and the new capabilities that arise when we combine certain components. But perhaps no digital alchemy is as powerful as when we combine an app-based platform with enterprise listening.

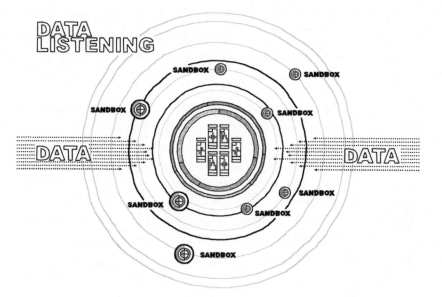

Here's why: Data listening is about building a central listener where anyone can plug into the stream of data being collected in real time. This automated system gathers data into a central place—a central listener—that can be accessed by anyone. The idea is to give any developer a very simple application programming interface (API) that provides access to the listener (the technophiles among you will recognize RESTful interfaces and JSON data structures as options here).

If you're a developer or team, you can register on a listener and get an API key. Next, you get back a one-liner in all of the languages you use. Once you copy and paste this into the code of your systems, you're able to specify the kind of data you want to listen to. The system then emits that data based on your API key so you have inherent lineage, which means you're able to look at data and easily identify where it came from. With the proper permissions and access, the user can scale up the resources or select another streaming data source. The ideal listening platform must also let anybody with a key say where he or she wants that data deposited and make it easy to point it there.

Throughout, functions remain seamless and automatic; we're talking about listeners that push in data automatically, before users even know they'll need to ask for it. Even if we're in an enterprise-grade management structure (let's say a petabyte of data a day, or more), we can manage capacity in seamless ways if we follow the same kind of automatic provisioning methods we laid out in Chapter 3 for the virtual data mart (VDM). Remember back then how we made it easy for people to provision a VDM? We designated access for a limited amount of time, but we also made it easy for them to ask for more time.

Similarly, here, we make it easy for developers to access capacity on the listener, with such capacity limited but easy to upgrade. Just like when a VDM user asks for more time, when a developer working with one gigabyte of data a day on the listener suddenly asks for 10 terabytes a day, that's your sign that this developer's little corner of the Analytical Application Platform just got more interesting. Based on the AonA we perform on these provisioning and usage patterns in the listener, we can direct our IT support teams to the apps that are potentially most valuable.

SETUP FOR SENTIENCE

By now you should be seeing a pattern of déjà vu moments, where seamless and agile dynamics around things like governance, provisioning, social conventions, and AonA keep reappearing throughout the five stages and remain applicable even as we scale the size and complexity of our systems.

This is not an accident. In fact, it's the key to why the Sentient Enterprise model works. We have decomposed enterprise analytics down to a manageable set of important contours and priorities that define an agile system. We're then taking care to build our web of people, processes, and technologies in accordance with this agile environment.

Stage 4 has given us the gift of action, of being able to scale our processes and work flows along with our insights. But this doesn't mean we've reached the point of getting the company to act as a single organism where the right hand intuitively knows what the left hand is doing. That's why any competitive business in the future needs to take things further—to be proactive and ensure that all these insights and actions are coordinated. Otherwise, we won't be very good at identifying micro trends, signaling the next big crisis, or capitalizing on the next new market opportunity.

For this kind of performance and coordination, the agile business needs to adopt autonomous decisioning at scale, delegating strategic thinking to people and leaving the grunt work to algorithms. That's what we're headed to in Stage 5, as we build the Autonomous Decisioning Platform.

CHAPTER 7

The Autonomous Decisioning Platform

ithin the past couple of years, each of your coauthors happened to buy a new car from Tesla, the forward-thinking company mentioned in Chapter 1's discussion on disruptive innovation. In comparing notes, it turns out we both were sold on the Tesla Autopilot feature that enables the car to steer itself within a lane, change lanes with the simple tap of a turn signal, and manage speed variations via traffic-aware cruise control.

The capabilities are such that we, as drivers, still ultimately need to handle most of the vehicle's operation. But the days are numbered before cars can truly drive themselves—sensing their environment, anticipating changes in circumstances, and making their own decisions about what to do next. The days are also numbered before an entire company can use analytics to do pretty much the same thing.

This chapter brings us to the Autonomous Decisioning Platform, the fifth and final stage of our Sentient Enterprise capability maturity model journey. Here, our objective is to position the enterprise in such a way that analytic algorithms are navigating circumstances and making the bulk of operational decisions without human help.

In light of this goal, we believe self-driving cars merit closer scrutiny. That's because the end state of having a fully autonomous vehicle involves a level of sentience not unlike what happens on the macro level for an entire organization as we approach the end state in our Sentient Enterprise journey.

FIVE STAGES

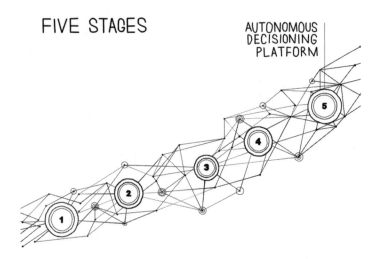

AUTONOMOUS
DECISIONING
PLATFORM

FAST-CHANGING CAPABILITIES

Autonomous drive—cars and trucks that pilot themselves—is perhaps the most rapidly maturing area of technology today. Even for industry veterans like Volvo's senior director of business analytics, Jan Wassen, the rate of progress is remarkable.

"I've been at Volvo since 1984 and have had lots of different roles in the company. In the late 2000s, I was working with a team dedicated to safety electronics like braking assist and lane monitoring for drowsiness detection," Jan told us in an interview from his office at Volvo's headquarters in Gothenburg, Sweden. "After moving to another department within the company, I returned to see a presentation by my old team a couple of years later and saw just how far these point solutions had since multiplied and evolved into a unified web of capabilities that together are making autonomous drive a reality."

Volvo's journey toward autonomous drive is built on a series of innovations, including the launch several years ago of the "connected car," which uses cloud-based technology to let vehicles share real-time safety and performance data with the company. Then, in 2016, Volvo debuted car-to-car communications (enabled by the connectivity cloud) designed to allow vehicles to share information like road and traffic conditions with each other.

"When you're in the middle of trying to innovate, you're spending all your time working to solve technical or logistical problems," added Bertil Angtorp, a senior strategy architect for information management and analytics at Volvo. "It's only when you step back and realize the big picture that you see how all these capabilities—some for safety, some for customer convenience—create an entirely new landscape for what's possible."

Supported by increasingly advanced sensors, connectivity, and artificial intelligence, Volvo's steps thus far are akin to our previous stages of the Sentient Enterprise; they've laid the foundation for the true sentience and autonomous decisioning that comes next. Indeed, as part of its Drive Me program, Volvo intends to have its first fully "unsupervised autonomous" vehicle—where the car is totally in control and totally responsible for the driving experience—available for sale to the public by 2021.

For all the excitement and progress, however, achieving the amount of sentience needed for unsupervised autonomous drive—or autonomous decisioning in the enterprise, for that matter—is a big threshold that can be crossed only with high levels of confidence in the underlying analytics and systems all working together in concert.

SELF-DRIVING CARS . . . AND COMPANIES

Let's take an even closer look at the technology and collaborative innovation required for autonomous drive. That's because, as we previewed in Chapter 4, if you understand the complex foundation and interplay of various technologies and systems that go into a self-driving car, you're on the way to seeing what needs to happen at a macro level for an entire organization to become a Sentient Enterprise.

Algorithms are behind the complex artificial intelligence (AI) systems that now let cars—properly equipped with sensors, navigation, and connectivity features—to drive and make countless traffic decisions all by themselves. Some of the best innovations arise from partnerships between traditional manufacturers and technology companies. Besides its own Drive Me projects in Sweden, Britain, and China, for instance, Volvo supplies its connected XC90 SUVs for Uber's self-driving tests in Pittsburgh, Pennsylvania, and Tempe, Arizona.

While Volvo is certainly a leader in the push for self-driving cars, it's by no means alone. As this book went to press, there were no fewer than six major auto manufacturers—Volvo, General Motors, Ford, Tesla, Fiat Chrysler, and Honda—investing sizable resources in autonomous vehicles. While the areas of focus may vary—from GM, Ford, and Volvo's investment in taxi and ride-hailing services, to Tesla's ongoing Autopilot upgrades and Honda's AI-driven "emotion engine" program to help cars "learn" from the driver's judgments and anticipate future decisions—the shared objective is to jockey for dominance in a vast and brand new market that's just now coming within reach.

Again, we must stress the importance of partnerships across a network of auto makers, suppliers, and technology firms responsible for many different systems and capabilities. Besides the Volvo/Uber collaboration, there's the GM/Lyft alliance for self-driving taxis, Ford's $1 billion investment in Argo AI and Fiat Chrysler's partnership with Alphabet, just to name a few. Such collaborations are necessary to achieve the complex mixture of perception, prediction, and motion planning needed in order for the car to drive and make decisions on its own.

Perception involves understanding what the car sees: is that another car, a traffic light, a pedestrian? Prediction helps the car understand what will likely happen next: Will that other car change lanes? Is that traffic light about to change? Will that person enter the crosswalk? And motion planning involves decisions and task execution: Should we change lanes? Should we stop? Should we make a turn?

All of this functionality needs to happen at speed and in the context of the rider experience. Was the ride smooth? Did the car take a turn too quickly or tailgate other cars too closely? The car's decisions and execution must be at least as good as, and hopefully better than, what a human driver is able to do.

This level of performance represents a very high bar to achieve. In fact, neither technology nor the law has yet reached the point where a self-driving car can truly be unsupervised or have what widely accepted international standards consider "full automation," in which the people on board the vehicle are no longer expected to have responsibility for what the car does. For that to happen, the resources for perception, prediction, and motion planning will need to keep improving, along with systems integration and processing power.

"We're looking at connectivity, adaptability to road conditions, and how sensors operate in bad weather," explains Volvo's Jan Wassen. "Sheer electrical power is another big challenge: the car has to have enough power for all the sensors, radar, and computational processing that needs to happen at highway speeds. But the systems keep getting better, and we're on track to succeed."

"SYSTEM OF SYSTEMS" BUILDING BLOCKS FOR SENTIENCE

Volvo and the many other companies we mentioned are leveraging what's become known as a system of systems approach to technological progress. It's what lets you create a world-changing innovation that is more than the simple accumulation of all the smart systems (braking, acceleration, steering, perception, motion planning, etc.) that went into it. Just like a self-driving car, a Sentient Enterprise reaches these advanced levels of awareness and autonomous decisioning through seamless integration of various different analytic processes and architectures—various systems—within the organization.

Think back to how we first adopted the Layered Data Architecture, built the virtual data marts in the Agile Data Platform, and then harmonized varied streams of data to clarify patterns and value within the Behavioral Data Platform. From these foundational steps, we enabled LinkedIn for Analytics within the Collaborative Ideation Platform. Upon that system, we built the more advanced Analytical Application Platform to package up the complexity and enable people to "like," "share," and "follow" not just data sets, but entire analytic processes and algorithmically driven work flows.

When we reach Stage 5, however, our ability to use algorithms to actually make independent decisions now elevates the company to a fundamentally new way of operating. It's not magic, but it is transformative—the same way it's transformative when the accumulation of automated subsystems in a vehicle reaches the tipping point where the self-driving car is born. Our Sentient Enterprise is now so self-aware and proactive that it can predict and adapt to changing circumstances, able to sense micro trends and make many decisions without human intervention.

ALGORITHMS: A MUST-HAVE FOR AUTONOMOUS DECISIONING

Picture the absolute thrill of monitoring and strategically intervening as your business acts as one organism: self-aware, proactive, able to sense micro trends around the next corner, and able to signal the next crisis or the next new thing and respond quickly, with smart strategies to prepare and optimize performance as circumstances inevitably change.

What has to happen in Stage 5 to make this attractive picture a reality? To begin with, we must understand how the nature of decision making in a modern, data-intensive business has fundamentally changed—evolved, really—to the point where we absolutely need algorithmic help to keep up with the flood of decisions to be made. It's no longer a choice to use algorithmic intelligence; it's a mandate!

A modern data environment is like a factory where, when you change the speed of one set of machines, it rocks the flow of everything else. With data, any advance can potentially drive a complex ripple effect of change and complexity throughout the company. In this environment, algorithms, and the grunt work they perform doing calculations, data processing, and automated reasoning, are not just nice options for help with decision making; they're absolutely essential!

These algorithms are embodied in intelligent agents; able to see, sense and control everything humans can—understanding imagery and identifying objects within that imagery, using computer peripherals such as a mouse or keyboard, or virtually any other task that a human can perform via development of generalized problem solving skills through training on different types of data. Eventually, intelligent agents can apply these skills to other domains and quickly infer and reason through mechanisms of transfer learning. Transfer learning applies general purpose machine intelligence into new environments and offers a very compelling future for machines to drive autonomous decision making.

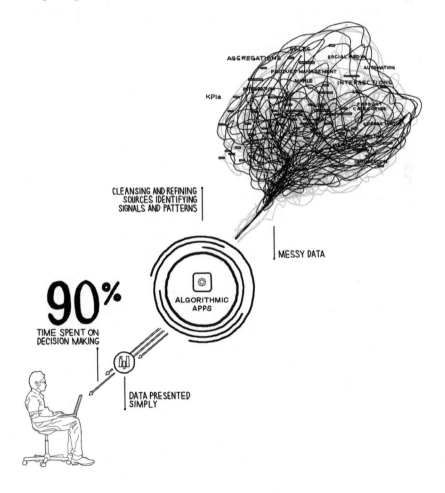

Let's look at what used to be a simple example to see how this works:

Retail has weathered many unpredictable changes over the centuries, but one fairly predictable change from year to year is the varied length of shopping days between Thanksgiving and Christmas. Congress decreed in 1941 that Thanksgiving fall on the fourth Thursday of November. So, for nearly eight decades, retailers have been able to rely on a predictable cadence that—cycling every several years—alternates the time from as few as 26 to as many as 32 days between Thanksgiving and the December 25 Christmas holiday.

Even though the fluctuations are predictable, the situation remains complicated. Retailers must consider how the time difference may change customer behaviors. (Is that extra Sunday good or bad for business? Will people buy differently, or perhaps take that extra time to travel versus spend the time and money shopping?) The industry also must decide on things like the timing of marketing campaigns, staffing for the holiday rush, and—critically—how best to stock and ship merchandize.

Now consider how a single change in one competitor's shipping capacity makes things infinitely more complicated. In 2015, online retailer Amazon began offering Prime Now shipping service that promises one- to two-hour delivery. That's a change not just in what Amazon can offer, but in how competitors must respond (to match shipping and/or beat pricing, and so on) and how customers' behavior may be altered as a result of expedited shipping. A complex domino chain of decisions throughout the enterprise follows.

Our message here is that the more velocity and innovation in an industry, the more difficult it is for humans to keep up with decisions that must be made. Every change introduces more complexity in addition to more data to the point where you no longer have enough people to keep track of everything. Let's not forget this example deals with just two major variables or dimensions: a competitor's shipping innovation and the fluctuation in days between holidays. Even this situation, given we're operating at scale, is already far too complicated for algorithms *not* to take over most of the decisioning.

Dimensions are those facts and measures we use to answer business questions. Some of the most common dimensions are people, products, place, and time. At a recent IoT Hackathon in San Diego, however, we saw participants try to solve a 42-dimensional problem. It's hard enough for a human data scientist to get his or her head around a seven-dimensional business problem, let alone one with 42 dimensions. With big data, this kind of complexity happens all the time, and algorithms are absolutely essential to making decisions about which dimensions to eliminate, manage, or tee up for human attention.

We've already seen in Chapter 4 how behavioral data swells the variety of information we contend with today—everything from demographics and geographic location to buying behavior and social media sentiment. Every one of those is a dimension that runs through vast volumes of data, to the point where it's simply impossible for people to keep track. Humans simply can't do it. But algorithms can!

STRATEGICALLY APPLYING ALGORITHMIC INTELLIGENCE IN THE ENTERPRISE

As we make our enterprise more self-aware and autonomous, intelligent agents demonstrating algorithmic intelligence and machine learning are the engines that drive the process. We are already seeing algorithmic intelligence applied to some business settings in ways that are more effective than any human could match.

Such intelligence is a major area of research for high-frequency stock trading, for instance, with algorithms now able to predict stock price fluctuations down to the last millisecond. In manufacturing, many quality control decisions are made by algorithms. Particularly when environmental conditions are key (sterile settings needed for chip manufacturing or pharmaceutical production, for instance), you pretty much have no choice but to run algorithms to efficiently measure and regulate humidity, temperature, air particulate, and related factors.

Algorithmic intelligence is being applied in even more sophisticated ways to e-commerce, as our recent Amazon shipping example demonstrates. Algorithms are what are behind that company's ability to now offer one- to two-hour shipping in some areas—anticipating what and where people will buy, and prepositioning merchandise accordingly. In fact, during a productivity discussion on Amazon's Q2

2015 earnings call, CFO Brian Olsavsky said, "We're using software and algorithms to make decisions, rather than people, which we think is more efficient and scales better and will be more accurate."

For every established use, like expedited shipping in retail, many others will keep coming to mind. Imagine, for instance, prepositioning algorithms revolutionizing delivery of lifesaving medications during an epidemic, particularly if you commingle public health data tracking how an outbreak is spreading.

More and more sophisticated use cases like this are made possible by the continued growth of machine learning. While a $1,000 laptop today can think at roughly the speed of a mouse (a real mouse, that is), in 2023 it will be able to compute at the speed of one human brain—in other words, at the speed of thought. Chip sets today drive around 0.1 trillion operations per second but with GPGPU and Tensor Flow chips we see a future where 165 quadrillion operations per second are possible. This will drive artificial intelligence, algorithmic intelligence and machine learning to new levels and is already enabling businesses to practically predict the future.

Consider this example: A new partnership between BP and GE's Intelligent Platforms unit is connecting 650 wells to the industrial Internet, employing machine learning to predict maintenance failures and repair needs. The goal is to get unplanned downtime as close to zero as possible, an important priority in light of the estimated $3 million a company loses in revenue per week when a well breaks down. As GE oil and gas director of product management Bob Judge summarized, "Telling a customer what to fix after it has failed is relatively easy. Telling them to fix something before it costs them money is the magic."

ALGORITHMIC "MAGIC"

By that reckoning, Siemens is creating magic worldwide on a daily basis. Powerful algorithms are behind the predictive and preventive maintenance analytics Gerhard Kress first told us about in Chapter 2—allowing the company to maintain a global network of wind turbines, traffic controls, medical devices, locomotives, and some 300,000 other connected devices.

As Siemens Mobility's vice president of data services, Gerhard is focused on energy and service efficiencies in rail systems on behalf of clients. There are even some customers who simply rent locomotives and leave the entire supply chain and service ecosystem for Siemens to manage—in effect, making Siemens its own customer!

Gerhard discussed his job using data to answer questions like when a part may fail, whether to repair or replace a part, and how to optimize the supply chain to get parts where they need to be in time so the fix is as proactive as the find:

"There are gearboxes, for example, on high-speed trains. They are tricky to monitor. We had a couple of cases where we could predict those things would be breaking in a few weeks. We had ample time to provide the spare parts, get the train in, repair it without harming the schedule, and work with the customer without creating any problems for them. Everything is connected on a network to an integrated platform—a data lake—and that platform understands where data is, can move it, shuffle it around. We have machine learning to help identify false positives and give a clear prediction of actual part failures. There can easily be more false alarms in this business than real alarms. So we look at work orders, serial numbers, the history of train and service data, diagnostic data, sensor data, repair processes, and supply chain data to help identify and resolve the real alarms."

We've stressed elsewhere how never to lose sight of the real-world impact and customer value that should be the driving force for your analytics. In this case, given how on-time arrivals mean everything to customers, Siemens helped one high-speed line between Barcelona and Madrid achieve reliability to the point where only one in 2,000 trains experienced anything more than a five-minute delay. This, in turn, gave the carrier confidence to offer full refunds to any traveler delayed more than 15 minutes—a huge differentiator that boosted ridership significantly.

ANALYTICS ON ALGORITHMS TO IMPROVE DECISION MAKING

Previous stages talked about analytics on analytics (AonA). Especially now that we're in the realm of needing algorithms to manage and make decisions from signal detection—raising signals out of the noise that comes with big data at scale—we need what we call Analytics on Algorithms to make sure our algorithms make the right decisions. Put simply: What if our algorithms start getting it wrong?

The truth is that algorithms are not perfect; they can screw up or be fooled by certain unusual or changing circumstances, or lack of the right data. Consider the simple example of a smart home that alters lighting, heat, and other household systems depending on the environment and occupancy. Those algorithms running the smart home system can sometimes get confused, especially in situations where there may be time lags involved—say, the period between turning up the thermostat and actually getting the house to that temperature. Perhaps it's been a cloudy day, but now it's getting nice out and sunlight through the windows speeds up heating. In such cases, you can see algorithms oscillate, undershooting or overshooting control decisions.

In keeping with the systems on systems approach we outlined earlier in this chapter, we are indeed applying the same agile AonA methodology we utilized in earlier stages. Only now we're applying analytics not just on data sets or work flow applications, but on entire algorithms!

With Analytics on Algorithms, we examine how algorithms behave and train them to make decisions the way we want them to be made. It's almost as if the data scientists on our AonA team are having an ongoing conversation with the algorithms. ("Hey, algorithm, you're tending to make decisions the wrong way, or you're doing it wrong when you're dealing with data sets that are bigger than X. Here's a better way to make decisions in that situation.")

The humans on the AonA team, in other words, are like guides and tutors to help algorithms do their best jobs possible. Even a well-functioning algorithm needs a certain amount of training, especially when it's first created and put to work. Think back to the Tesla Autopilot analogy. There's a break-in period where the company urges you to do most of the driving while Autopilot learns your way of doing things.

Beyond that, there will always be moments where you need human intervention. Autopilot can get stumped by missing lane markers and at some intersections that feature irregular turns or gradients; and the system can't make the kind of judgment calls you need when you're at a four-way stop, with three other drivers trying to decide who goes next. Self-driving taxis, meanwhile, have been known to run red lights and even get in accidents. Analytics on Algorithms in the enterprise allows tweaks and guidance from humans to help algorithms get through situations where they tend to screw up on their own.

Humans should take heart in this, especially those worried about a Terminator-style "Skynet" or some menacing "singularity" or "strong AI," where systems redesign and improve themselves to the point where humans are obsolete. As we made clear earlier in this chapter, algorithms can indeed monitor and multitask decisions in ways that humans can never match. But they won't be able to do so without humans anytime soon for critical interventions and strategic decisions.

"As algorithms take over more of the decision making, these new systems will still require people, those who have very advanced skills who can train the algorithms," said Jacek Becla, Teradata's vice president for technology and innovation, whom we first met in Chapter 4. But Jacek argued that the enduring role of humans will create new challenges of their own.

"These people will have enormous power, and that in and of itself creates a whole new class of problems," Jacek explained. "When you train algorithms, you have a lot of responsibility for security and even the ethics around how you're setting up the algorithms to make what might be life-or-death decisions." Jacek offered the scenario, thankfully still a hypothetical, of an autonomous vehicle that may have to decide whether to hit a brick wall, which may kill the driver, instead of a crowd of bystanders, which may involve multiple fatalities.

"There's no job description today that approximates this responsibility, except perhaps military commanders or the president of a country. But that kind of awesome responsibility will soon be in the purview of advanced data scientists," Jacek summarized. "It's uncharted territory, but things are going in that direction and we're going to have to figure out how to handle this new class of problem."

COMBINING ALGORITHMS ON THE HOME STRETCH TO SENTIENCE

As we get better at building algorithms, we see our autonomous decisioning capabilities improve. And as we learn to share and optimize algorithmic intelligence throughout the enterprise, we get better at making various algorithms work together—at connecting systems together with other systems to approach that true inflection point where the enterprise becomes "sentient."

This would be the point where the organization is essentially self-aware, where one hand knows what the other is doing, almost like a single organism that can sense conditions and be proactive with trends, forecasts, decisions, and strategies. In the process, you speed past many of the previous roadblocks we've talked about in this book.

No longer are your people stuck sifting through data 90 percent of the workday, with only 10 percent of their time spent making decisions; now that ratio is reversed. No longer is it only humans who can identify patterns when they glance at a chart or examine a data set. Now our analytic systems can see changes in patterns, spot aberrations in data, find the exceptions, make the easy decisions, and flag the more important decisions—along with the most relevant information—for humans to handle.

Think back to the frustrating story we shared in Chapter 2 about the telecommunications CFO preparing for a Q4 earnings call as her team couldn't begin to explain a five percent revenue drop, or whether that number was even accurate. Let's revisit that opening story and see how things might be different if this were a Sentient Enterprise:

> In the Sentient Enterprise, the CFO does not miss that initial event ultimately leading to the sales revenue dip. All the components we built in Stages 1 through 5 are working seamlessly together to help the enterprise isolate the cause upstream in the process. This allows us to mitigate the problem before that tiny wave can ever become a tsunami of problems and confused questions.
>
> Long before the Q4 earnings call, back in Q1, a consumer satisfaction index app alerts the business analyst team that customer sentiment is turning negative. The analysts enter natural language questions into a collaboration platform to pull from loosely coupled and noncoupled data. These are questions like: "Where are the highest contract cancellations in the past 30 days?" or "What are the various paths that customers took before canceling?"

This team posts its findings on the Collaborative Ideation Platform and asks if anyone has ideas for what's behind the dip. Analysts and engineers from different teams and offices around the world chime in and post findings from their own investigations. Someone mentions social media chatter around a competitor's discount coupon program in several U.S. urban areas with a history of customer complaints about dropped calls by the company. The team cross-checks this data with the revenue decline and sees a strong connection.

The analysts rank all the different possibilities (including the possibility that this is really all about the winter weather) and settle on this competitor discount program as the number-one hypothesis to test first. The analysts collaborate with the marketing department, which creates a targeted e-mail campaign to customers who are likely to be dissatisfied with their phone service in the past 15 days and have been exposed to the competitor's discount coupon campaign.

The campaign succeeds in keeping 85 percent of the customers, and the marketing department rolls it out broadly. It turns out that in good weather or bad, customers can still be convinced to stick around. When Q4 earnings come in that year, sales and revenue are both up significantly, and the company's stock sails upward. The crisis is averted!

This is a very different outcome from the not-so-hypothetical headache we laid out in Chapter 2! These two stories illustrate the benefits of moving from a reactive company to a proactive, algorithmically driven enterprise that identifies threats and opportunities long before they become obvious.

AGILITY AS THE ULTIMATE LITMUS TEST

If we've successfully made our way through all five stages of this Sentient Enterprise capability maturity model, we should have an enterprise that's able to make more strategic decisions based on a better understanding of both the breadth and the depth of data at our disposal. Instead of simply telling data what it should do, we can finally let data do more of the talking.

That said, every company is different. Your own particular journey through the stages will have its own peaks and valleys, its own landscape of opportunities and challenges. That's why our next chapter on charting your own course is structured as a tool kit of sorts. It's a modular list of issues and dynamics you'll likely encounter as you seek to implement the five-stage approach in your own organization. As you apply the concepts in this book to your own real-world business environment, remember the mantra we set out in Stage 1: to align people, processes, and technology in service of agility around data.

You'll no doubt encounter plenty of specific situations and challenges in your company for which there's not a specific answer laid out in this book. In those situations, remember that the ultimate litmus test is whether we've stayed agile as we scale the enterprise. Everything you do should be in service of agility: to establish it, build on it, and amplify it. If anything happens along the way that detracts from agility, then something's wrong. Nothing else matters nearly as much as agility.

CHAPTER 8

Implementing Your Course to Sentience

Now that we've walked through the stages of the Sentient Enterprise journey, you can see how this approach is designed to apply broadly to many different kinds of companies scaling their analytic architectures to grow bigger, more autonomous, and more agile. The flip side of this broad applicability, however, is there's no single way to go about implementing this capability maturity model. Nor is it completely sequential.

As we stressed way back in our Introduction, it's possible to embrace different themes simultaneously, or even out of sequence, depending on your organizational structure and business needs. And however you organize it, the sheer scope of your to-do list can be daunting. In fact, after hearing us talk at a seminar about the Sentient Enterprise journey and all that's involved, one panicked executive at a major corporation buttonholed us to say she felt like she was at sea level looking up at Mount Everest.

She made a good point, and our reply was that even Mount Everest is tackled incrementally, in phases. Everest has more than a dozen routes to the summit, in fact, with a base camp and four other major camps along the way. The Sentient Enterprise journey is also doable if we look at it the same way, in phases. Our rattled executive can also take heart from those who are already well on their way up the mountain. "Of course, when you look at the beginning, it looks very hard," said Siemens Mobility's Gerhard Kress. "The only thing you can do is dive in and get started somewhere."

More than anything else, creating the Sentient Enterprise involves a tremendous amount of change management that goes far beyond anything you could capture in an employee handbook or the typical strategic plan. Your job is to put an entire culture shift into action at an established company, with fiefdoms to engage and IT policies to overcome. We've already shared with you the "change management on steroids" shorthand we use to describe the journey at conferences and companies around the world. There is simply no other way to describe it, and there's just no single way to go about it.

We won't prescribe a single path to sentience, because every company is different and must uniquely tailor the journey to its own unique history, culture, operations, challenges, and goals for the future. That said, we can show you some very common and practical considerations that most businesses will face along this journey.

To that end, we've structured this chapter as a kind of guided tour of some important and interrelated priorities to keep in mind as you implement. These are some of the major signposts as you drive your organization's analytics capabilities along a path to sentience and maturity.

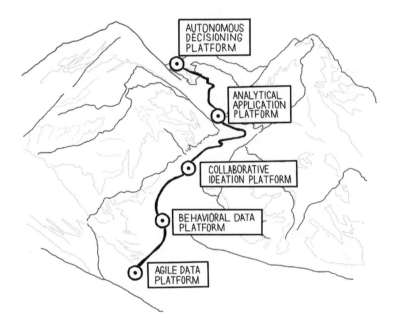

ASK THE RIGHT QUESTIONS, WARTS AND ALL

Making real progress starts with a candid assessment of where you are currently. Let's be honest: these moments of recognition can be incredibly uncomfortable. When we finish talking about the Sentient Enterprise to a roomful of business executives, we invariably have people approach us afterward who are literally in shock, saying things like: "Oh my gosh, we are so behind the curve. Where do we start?" Our answer is that, by realizing the challenge, you've already started; the next step is to ask straightforward and honest questions of your business.

Where are the silos and hurdles to agility? What are the policies around copying data? Is our funding structured for innovation and adaptation to new opportunities? How do we recruit, train, manage, and retain our data professionals? These are just a few questions you need to include in a "warts and all" checklist that is a crucial first step toward changing things for the better.

As you might guess, the navel-gazing doesn't usually go well when done solely from within the company. That's why we recommend you invest in an agility audit. This kind of organizational review is best done by an outside party with no biases or political ties to your company to help establish an independent, baseline assessment of how agile your analytics operations and processes currently are. The audit should be thorough and company-wide, with resulting collateral like presentations, training, and a road map for change that includes future steps toward agility.

A good agility audit will feature an itemized and prioritized backlog of current issues and tasks that need addressing. The list should include some early wins—changes that can be made quickly and fairly easily—along with more far-reaching transitions that may require months or even years to implement. The entire process can help you socialize and expand on practices and areas where your company is agile, and remedy those areas where agility lags.

AGILE STRATEGIC PLANNING IS *NOT* AN OXYMORON

Many established strategic planning approaches you've learned about for years in business school are perfectly good ones that remain relevant today. It always makes sense, for instance, to define goals, set direction, and make decisions on allocating resources in pursuit of a strategy. It's also a great idea to measure results and have flexibility for both planned and emergent events as you compete and adapt to market environments.

However, big data has changed one factor—timing—in a way that has upended the whole notion of strategic planning and how we should go about it. Technology has helped speed enterprise production to the point where some industries operate on a three-week product release cycle. In such a fast-paced and data-enhanced world of rapid resourcing and action, it doesn't make sense to have all your strategic planning happening on a two- or three-year rhythm, with reliance on long-term waterfall methodologies that simply don't apply in today's world.

As we discussed in Chapter 3, waterfall methodologies are step-by-step approaches that may be fine in cases where you have a clear picture of what your final outcome should be, and time to completion is not a big deal. Those two conditions alone, however, are non-starters when you consider the role analytics needs to play in today's competitive markets. Most companies nonetheless stick with outdated waterfall playbooks from a less agile era. This leaves them stuck with micro-incremental product improvements and vulnerability to competitors that understand that bolder and more disruptive improvements are what now drive competitive advantage.

Your strategic planning processes must recognize this reality, and the Sentient Enterprise journey requires we update to a more agile and opportunity-driven framework. Think, for example, of how financial options work or how movie studios strategically bankroll many productions concurrently in hopes that a few efforts will pay off big. We need to pivot the enterprise to strategically invest in similarly agile ways.

At the same time, we can't ignore the basic financial realities that come with being a large company. Especially for publicly traded firms, for example, strict annual and quarterly budgeting processes are a fact of life. No amount of cheerleading for agility can change that. But compromises are possible. Consider designating annual or quarterly-funded programs that, in turn, feature flexible allocation models internally that sponsor a handful of short-term projects happening concurrently or in quick succession.

These sprints can be pilot efforts where program or project managers can track progress in shorter increments—a week or two of work, say—using measures like net present value and other real-time snapshots on return on investment (ROI) and profitability. It's the kind of agile, opportunity-driven approach that dovetails with our next suggestion: that you view your analytics team almost like a venture-backed entrepreneurial team within your own company.

ADOPT A START-UP MIND-SET AND DON'T
BOIL THE OCEAN

It's easy for a start-up to be agile; it's almost a given when you're new, small, and hungry for results. But larger enterprises can get caught up in bloated procedures, legacy systems, static financing, workforce issues, and other barriers to agility.

Our advice: don't try to "boil the ocean" by taking on the whole company at once in your pursuit of agility. We have a tremendous challenge in front of us, but we can take it in steps. The way to do this is to start thinking of yourself and your analytics team as a kind of venture capital-driven start-up team within your own company.

Here's what we mean by that: Instead of trying to fix the whole company at once, pick a key area or two where some business problem happens be a good candidate for a particular analytics solution you're working on. Find partners who are close enough to the problem that they're desperate for your solution and are willing to act as validators at staff meetings, budget sessions, or anywhere else you need buy-in. The more you can limit the scope of these early pockets of agility, the more quickly you can scale success within them to demonstrate what works best.

If these targeted and value-driven strategic engagements inside the company resemble how a start-up operates out in the real world, that's exactly the point! In fact, try to look at internal partners as those "lighthouse customers" we mentioned in Chapter 6—internal divisions or departments whose business problems make up a kind of venture portfolio within the company. Focus on these pockets of agility and peg success to milestones. Use short-term performance indicators to spot early wins or pitfalls so you can know which projects to highlight and keep pursuing, tweak, or abandon.

As for time lines, condense them in a "fail fast, recover fast" approach where you focus like a hawk on one or two things for a month, maybe two, and then adjust your approach based on a granular understanding of what worked and what didn't. This is much better than trying to monitor a bunch of outcomes over the course of a year or more. Wherever possible, in fact, look for business problems with natural limitations around scope and time frame. This is good advice, even for established analytics leaders looking to refine or test new approaches.

For instance, Verizon Wireless mounted a proof of concept for better predictive modeling around customer churn in its prepay division; the goal was to examine behaviors and decide which customers to target most aggressively for retention. Verizon focused on the 30- to 60-day window after a prepay balance hits zero, during which time the company holds the phone number in limbo just in case the customer decides to replenish the account. The built-in limitations—prepay customers only, and that built-in 30- to 60-day time box before releasing the number—served as natural contours to help focus and pilot a new (and ultimately successful) analytic approach for the company.

PICK THE RIGHT INTERNAL PARTNERS TO DEMONSTRATE VALUE

Choosing these intracompany partnerships is not an exact science, but you can follow a few guidelines. Certain operations, like marketing, tend to work quickly and incrementally, with feedback loops built in; marketing campaigns tend to run on short cycles and measure progress often through surveys, social media, and other channels.

Such operations can be good candidates for a pilot project, since they tend to match the agile cadence of your analytics approach. Other parts of your company, like finance, may be more tethered to long-term cycles and measures and are therefore going to be tougher prospects for early wins.

Sometimes the same kind of operation will vary in suitability, depending on the business context. The pace of supply chain operations, for example, may be ripe for agile analytics in the case of just-in-time parts provision manufacturing, or in e-commerce. Other contexts, like supply chain operations at a government agency, could take additional effort to apply the venture approach to analytics.

Throughout, make sure to respect your partner department's expertise. Don't come in and tell them how to do their work; your job is more as a solutions provider whose goal is to share the philosophy and framework around agile analytics and show how this approach can work for them. As you rack up successes, take them viral throughout the company by finding bigger projects and/or seeding team members from successful efforts onto other teams that are gearing up for another pilot project somewhere else in the company.

EMBRACE AGILE PROJECT MANAGEMENT STRATEGIES

We've talked at great length about the use of platforms as a kind of framework to help users be agile in accessing, visualizing, or making decisions around data. But your analytics teams also need an agile framework of their own to set up these architectures in the first place. Big data demands fundamental changes not only in how we conceive agility, but how we actually carry it out in practical, everyday terms as we structure and build our data architectures.

Many organizations talk about agility but don't have the right tactical methodologies to follow through. Fortunately, as we mentioned in Chapter 3, agile project management platforms such as Scrum are already out there. And as we discussed in Chapter 6, the whole concept of DevOps is revolutionizing the agility and repeatability of analytics work flow and applications development.

Embrace iterative and incremental methodologies that challenge assumptions of waterfall and other traditional, sequential approaches to product development. Enable teams to self-organize through physical colocation or close online collaboration, with frequent (often daily) face-to-face communication among all team members.

Rely on user groups to share best practices and get training or certifications. One such group, the Scrum Alliance, summarizes the allure: "When was the last time you put 'collaborative, sane and enjoyable' in the same sentence with 'business goals'? You may not remember unless you already use Scrum, but with Scrum you can, indeed, enjoy your work again!" Agile project management improves not only the team experience, but also the work product by maximizing the team's ability to deliver quickly and respond to emerging requirements.

EMBRACE CONCURRENCY, ENSURE SCALABILITY

It's easy to be agile when you're a start-up with just a few employees and a vision. But what if you're a large enterprise with many employees, legacy systems, and a hardened culture that may be anything but agile? We need to keep the insights coming in the face of mushrooming data volumes at scale.

Agile methodologies aren't much good if you don't have the analytic heft to run them at scale. This is true whether you're talking about documentation, product management, supply chain, customer satisfaction, quality control, or any number of enterprise activities. Wherever we grow the business, we have both the techniques and infrastructure to support big data at scale. Otherwise we're just investing in bigger data streams as the insights float by unnoticed.

One of the biggest scalability challenges by far involves concurrency: the need for today's large enterprise to do many things at the same point in time. Consider how a major international bank today can have 18 billion events or more across all identified customers. Especially with complicated challenges like fraud prevention, you may need to deal with hundreds of thousands of events happening concurrently—things like teller interactions, online transfers, call center and e-mail traffic, ATM visits, account cancellations, and other occurrences. The payoff in a use case like this is huge if your systems and people can navigate all this information in real time. But, if the concurrency isn't there, your discovery teams and tools are stuck in linear mode.

Even in cases where there's adequate funding, too many organizational systems and processes continue to be built in uncoordinated ways. The resulting mismatch can feel a lot like driving your expensive new sports car on the Autobahn stuck in first gear: it's very frustrating, you don't get very far—and you still paid a lot for the experience.

DESIGN IN GOVERNANCE THAT'S SEAMLESS AND REPEATABLE

Scalability also drives our argument for making sure your governance is built early and seamlessly into your data analytics systems and architectures. Think back to our simple analogy in Chapter 6 about version control: When composing documents, Microsoft Word is a very good platform when writing a draft or sharing tracked changes with a colleague or two; but the process can get unwieldy and complicated if more people join the effort. Google Docs, on the other hand, manages version control automatically and effortlessly, even if you have many contributors.

When you're building analytical applications, as we did in Chapter 6, the governance and documentation should be seamless. The ultimate test for governance is whether the experience feels seamless and effortless for your end users, and that means governance must hold up at scale by being repeatable and hassle-free.

As another example, consider taxi reimbursements in the pre- and post-Uber eras. Reimbursement offices at large companies can get swamped with paper receipts (or scans of those receipts); or that documentation can remain hassle-free via Uber's automatic documentation online when people use that Internet-based ride-summoning service.

OPTIMIZE A WORKFORCE TO ACT FAST, FAIL FAST, AND SCALE FAST

Through the Layered Data Architecture, LinkedIn for Analytics, and related platforms, we've shown you ways to optimize collaboration around data. But ultimately, collaboration happens between people, and that means implementing the Sentient Enterprise can't become reality in your organization without close attention to the people who work there.

When hiring new talent, look for gifted and self-driven engineers— and look for proof of this beyond what people may claim on a resume. Certain companies have reputations for progressive approaches to analytics, so pay special attention to applicants who are coming from those organizations. Successful cloud companies, in particular, are good sources for talent. As we learned in Chapter 6, the cloud is all about agility, new tooling, and finding ways to scale products and services without scaling people. So look for folks who come from that background.

Visit GitHub when vetting candidates, or some other code repositories, to see if your candidate has self-published interesting projects or technical challenges. If you don't find anything, ask your candidate to go ahead and do something like that as part of the interview process. When someone asks, "What is GitHub?" or "Why would I do that?," it's time to move on to the next candidate.

That said, don't focus excessively on new hires. Getting your workforce where it needs to be is less about new minds than a new mind-set. Focus on the kind of people and skills you need on hand to innovate. Chances are that many of those people are already in your company and just waiting for an opportunity to lead or support change.

"IT'S THE CULTURE, STUPID"

Any of the aforementioned strategies need to happen with an overall culture shift in mind. We've talked a lot about the collaborative spirit and how to promote and protect that. Employees must be trained not to rely excessively on intuition, emotion, and anecdote-based decisions and instead start trusting the data. Intuition is great for ideas, but data is actual proof.

"One of the biggest challenges we face in moving the needle as fast as we want is finding the right people who both understand the data and build the models; that's a very unique skill set," said Dell's Jennifer Felch. "You can have the most incredible technology, but you also need people who are very comfortable with the data—the definitions, what math means, and how to handle distributions. Our challenge used to be: 'We don't have all the data.' Now it's: 'We have the data, but we need people with the skills to understand and make sense of it.'"

Data-driven decisioning stops us from relying too much on what we feel or think may be happening. Workers also need to understand which metrics matter most for the business, what decisions need to be driven by the data, and how to harness algorithms to make the most strategic decisions possible. This involves understanding the business context within which data correlations occur.

It's been said that agile is not something you do; it's something you become. With that in mind, make sure you have a solid system to promote agility at every turn: from how you communicate to employees and conduct company meetings to how you build your teams and run your campaigns. Ignore corporate culture at your peril: as famed management consultant and theorist Peter Drucker reportedly said, "Culture eats strategy for breakfast."

Conclusion

As we conclude our journey through the five-stage Sentient Enterprise capability maturity model, we'd like to leave you with a bit more perspective on how all this intensive work within your company will help you be a pathfinder and leader—a pioneer who takes your organization in the direction it needs to go to survive in an ever-changing, data-intensive world. This is a business book, after all. We're not talking just about innovation, but about competitive advantage!

THE ERGONOMICS OF DATA: REDEFINING HUMAN–DATA INTERACTION

The simple truth is that any enterprise hoping to endure more than five or 10 years into the future must absolutely leverage the flood of data rising all around so its workforce can thrive instead of drown. That's why so much of the Sentient Enterprise is about resources and techniques to optimize human–data interactions, and helping employees of all kinds find new ways to manage data.

In doing so, we've hoped to advance a leadership model for human productivity—namely ergonomics—as the modern workplace increasingly becomes defined by data (the term *ergonomics* is derived from the Greek word for work, *ergon*). It's a scientific discipline that arose in response to World War II and the grueling pace that a national mobilization of industry imposed on both factory workers and soldiers operating machinery on the battlefield.

Ergonomics can boost productivity, protect workers, and even save lives. Some aviation accidents are attributed to flawed console design, and an investigation into the 1979 Three Mile Island nuclear accident ascribed partial responsibility to poorly designed control room instrumentation. With the digital age came a new ergonomic focus on things like graphical user interface design, and ergonomics today has reached the frontier where we ask: How should humans best interact with data itself?

We hope the parts of our Sentient Enterprise that deal with the human component help answer this question. As we learned in Chapter 5's Collaborative Ideation Platform—with LinkedIn and Facebook-style social media conventions to help the organization understand which ideas, projects, and people get followed, liked, shared, and so on—the more we borrow from social everything, the more we tack our operations and interfaces toward the way humans already think and behave. What better way to embody the concept of ergonomics when it comes to data and analytics?

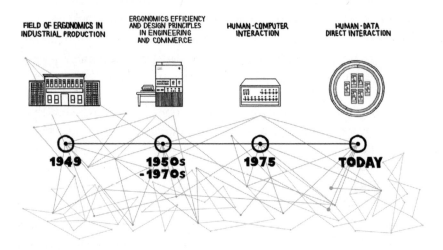

The social and gamification elements, for instance, are helping improve everything from metadata management to worker satisfaction and creativity. We're also learning which visualizations work best and how to tee up information for decision making in the most efficient way possible. These are the kinds of make-or-break skills the enterprise must master to keep pace with an ever-growing big data universe.

There is no single way to structure all of our big data and computing power. But, as we saw in Chapter 7, innovation, scalability, and industry breakthroughs seem to happen most dramatically within a "systems of systems" logic. Inside our enterprise, we adopted that same logic to build complex data architectures and systems on top of more foundational systems to scale our analytics and enhance agility.

Why do we innovate in this way? Because the entire world is starting to operate this way! We're making the enterprise compatible with tomorrow's global data architectures—plugging into the emerging reality of what data means to the world and how the world is using it. Those of us who do it first are the ones who will lead and gain the most competitive advantage.

SOCIETY-WIDE SYSTEM OF SYSTEMS ADOPTION

Our book stayed focused within the enterprise while leveraging the Internet of Things, behavioral data, and related big data elements. But there is absolutely no limit to how far we can take this alchemy of sensors, connections, analytics, and algorithms beyond the walls of any single company to create more and more complex systems and solutions for problems facing entire industries—even society at large.

The upshot: *The more our organization operates the way society will operate in the future, the better we'll be able to compete and thrive in that society.*

As a *Harvard Business Review* article on technology and competition pointed out, a dynamic system of systems approach can lead to tremendous industry-changing, and even world-changing, innovations. The article cites global agriculture—feeding the world's people—as a potent success story. Heavy machinery, irrigation systems, soil and nutrient sensors, financial information, and weather data are all connected and coordinated in ways that supercharge farm yields and efficiencies. (Go to https://hbr.org/2014/11/how-smart-connected-products-are-transforming-competition for the full article.)

As we mentioned in Chapter 7, self-driving cars represent another revolutionary system of systems innovation. Once we have our self-driving car, however, we'll eventually graduate to an even larger system of systems environment of many such cars coordinating with each other and with centralized networks governing traffic and roads for efficient and driverless transport on a massive scale.

Zoom out even further, and we're getting into "smart city" territory, where all sorts of civic infrastructure and functions are coordinated and optimized by IoT-driven analytics. The analyst firm IDC, in fact, has identified federal, state, and local government clients as leading IoT buyers, with compounded annual growth rates of more than 10 percent through 2017 and beyond. And IDC points to analytics-driven smart city applications that run the gamut from enhanced service delivery and crime prevention to smart water and lighting systems.

As just one example, the City of San Diego recently folded IoT innovation into what otherwise would have been routine upgrades to its network of street lights. When it came time for aging street lights to be replaced with more energy-efficient LED lights in the city's historic Gaslamp district, the city made sure to outfit some of the new lights with IoT sensor arrays—cameras, microphones, and related equipment—to track temperature, humidity, and other factors. Some processing is done "on the edge"—instantly at the source—and other data is analyzed in more centralized locations.

"We were replacing the street lights anyway," San Diego's chief digital officer, Maksim Pecherskiy, told us in an interview for this book. "And we wanted to add that additional smartness while we were at it." The resulting data is used for things like public safety and tracking pavement conditions for repair crews. In addition, computer vision algorithms can count car, bike, and pedestrian traffic, taking some of the guesswork out of efforts to increase bike ridership as part of San Diego's aggressive Climate Action Plan.

"I'm excited to be able to say, 'Well, we made this policy change. Has that decreased or increased the amount of bike ridership in the city?' Or else we can say, 'Let's see, we put this bike lane here; has that increased or decreased the amount of bike ridership?'" Maksim told us. "And so we can begin to really make these data-driven decisions, instead of just saying, 'Well, I think if we put a bike lane here, people will use it.'"

"Smart cities are smart to the extent that they're proactive," said Jay Nath, Maksim's counterpart some 450 miles north in San Francisco. Jay serves as the first city-level chief innovation officer in the country. With a background in private-sector start-ups, he's helping

San Francisco leverage analytics to predict and prevent things like house fires and homelessness.

"Much of government today is still very reactive: when there's a fire, we'll react to it; when someone becomes homeless, we'll react to it," Jay told us in an interview. "But we're asking ourselves: 'Why can't we anticipate and prevent?' So, for instance, data from previous housing code violations and other city records might tell us how to proactively visit a home to prevent a fire from happening in the first place."

One challenge, as we've seen elsewhere in this book, is interoperability. "San Francisco now has a Department of Homelessness that integrates and coordinates some 13 different data systems," Jay told us. "We need to know what our data inventory is; it's basic blocking and tackling, walk before you run kind of thing."

"I don't want city infrastructure to become a mesh of 15 different networks and 15 different protocols," echoed San Diego's Maksim Pecherskiy. "I want a base infrastructure and people to build on top of that platform."

This is just a snapshot of how analytics is revolutionizing not just business, but larger industry-wide and societal systems. It's a big picture reminder of why our work in analytics doesn't create just business value, but also civic value in our search to solve community and humanitarian challenges.

We hope this gives you some context for why we structured our Sentient Enterprise stages the way we did: you can position all the work we're doing inside the company as a system of systems strategy that aligns with a larger, global playbook for data-driven growth and progress. Such positioning allows your organization to fully leverage that broader landscape of growth and progress.

THE GREATER GOOD

Because the Sentient Enterprise is defining strategies that can revolutionize not just business, but larger industry-wide and societal systems, might some of these strategies enable solutions to larger community and humanitarian challenges? We took a look at smart cities and mentioned earlier how system of systems innovation is revolutionizing agriculture to help feed the world's people. In Chapter 7, we showed how algorithms that optimize Amazon's prepositioning of merchandise for one- to two-hour shipping could perhaps be used to prepositon medication as a disease outbreak spreads.

How many other innovations like this might be possible? And how can we ensure that we reap the benefits of technology and organizational sentience while minimizing the downsides? (After all, "sentience" didn't turn out so well for Winston Smith and his fellow citizens in George Orwell's *1984*.)

Questions can be fairly asked about the dark side of sentience, but we believe these concerns are minimized by many of the technological, policy, and market forces we've discussed throughout this book. Thankfully, cybersecurity and privacy principles are already solid fixtures both in the design of the platforms we advocate in the Sentient Enterprise and in today's policy and economic discourse; they should continue as enduring and visible priorities as the future continues to take shape.

As argued in Chapter 7, humans will likely always stay in ultimate control of algorithms, relegating a Terminator-style "Skynet" dystopia solidly to the realm of science fiction. And while there's certainly a risk for abuse that comes with the unprecedented capacity to peer into people's lives, remember our cautionary note in Chapter 4 about using behavioral data to understand customers in ways that are "customized without being creepy."

The public will always have their buying decisions, voting patterns, and other levers of influence to keep organizational sentience in check as a largely positive force in society. Even so, sentience and what eBay's president and CEO, Devin Wenig, calls today's "renaissance in artificial intelligence" is creating broad economic and workforce dynamics that must be addressed.

"We need serious public policy discussion on the impact on the workforce in the next ten years, when there are driverless cars and when nobody is washing windows," he wrote in an essay from the 2017 World Economic Forum meetings in Davos, Switzerland. "We have to reduce the growing global divide between those who feel like they are benefiting from the forces of technology … and those who feel shut out and left behind."

Wenig says key priorities should be retraining workers for the skills they'll need tomorrow and ensuring as many people as possible share in technology's benefits. He and others rightly argue that technological advancement is inevitable and that the answer—rather than trying to restrain technology—is to shape it.

LOOKING TO THE FUTURE

If our goal is to shape the evolution of technology, what might those contours be? As we bring our book to a close, we thought it'd be useful to share perspective from some of our interviewees on what the future holds for analytics. Here's their take on what lies ahead over the next decade or so:

Brett Vermette, director of big data infrastructure and engineering at General Motors:

> "I think in the not too distant future, we'll start to see organizations like ours address the extended enterprise, not just the internal enterprise. So as we see organizations become more agile and data-driven themselves, a further frontier will offer more seamless coordination more broadly with their larger environment—which, for us, could include joint venture partners, dealer networks, and supplier groups. That's another order of magnitude of complexity that goes beyond just the enterprise itself.
>
> There's also a larger issue of what I often refer to as delight becoming demand and experiment becoming expectation: I think we'll continue to see more capabilities, but we'll also see more realization that these capabilities are expected and required as data gets more and more critical to the operation of the business. You want data to be mission critical and you want it to be relevant; but that means you have a responsibility to keep developing the foundational capabilities and make sure you can support the demand."

Grace Hwang, executive director for business intelligence and advanced analytics at Verizon Wireless:

> "For me, the future is about getting to a stage where, before customers know there's a problem or issue, we will be able to proactively offer to meet their needs. So, hypothetically, let's say we know from your web traffic or a mobile app that you bought an airline ticket, and we see you're going to Europe. We'd like to be able to proactively tell you that—knowing where you're traveling—here are the best roaming programs for you to consider. Today, you do get a text from us when you land overseas to inform you that you're roaming and here is the price. But that's after the fact. Tomorrow is about being proactive to the point where both the company and the customer stay ahead of the curve in terms of having more choices and avoiding surprises or problems before they happen."

Jennifer Felch, vice president for enterprise services and order experience at Dell:

> "We're hopefully going to see companies get proactive to the point where, instead of measuring problems, we're measuring success. The new world is not going to be a big giant call center waiting for people to call and report problems. We'll be asking ourselves fewer questions like 'How fast was my response to the call?' or 'How quickly did I resolve the issue?' That's the legacy world. In the new world, you're looking at 'Why didn't I stop that problem before it started?' and 'How can I predict and prevent that negative event from happening in the first place?' I think this, combined with better capabilities to automate routine tasks and decisions, will free up more people and resources in your company to devote simply to talking with customers. And most of that time will be spent talking about opportunities and growth versus problems and troubleshooting."

Gerhard Kress, vice president of data services at Siemens Mobility:

> "Things are going to change dramatically. Data volumes will be a factor of probably a thousand times higher than

today, and you're going to have much more visibility into everything that's happening out in the field. Analytics will become the decisive factor for almost every reasonable decision. Analytics will drive decisions on every level, and there will be analytics of every kind to help customers improve the way their assets are being designed, engineered, produced, operated, and maintained in the future. Most of this will be unsupervised learning and deep learning technologies, so systems will start automating and improving on their own."

Jan Wassen, senior director of business analytics at Volvo:

"Obviously, for a company like mine, the future is going to continue to be about autonomous drive. All the testing and problem solving that's happening today will get us to the point where autonomous drive will be an ordinary reality, simply a fact of life. In fact, I believe the day will come when we're not allowed to drive ourselves any longer. Perhaps not every road, but for some major roads, you'll see autonomous drive as a requirement. We'll also see a lot more ride-sharing and fewer situations where there's only one person in the car, but the technology will be there to make that process easy and something people want to do. I think the future is going to involve a totally different ecosystem, where transportation by automobile is safer and more efficient."

Jacek Becla, vice president for technology and innovation at Teradata and former head of scalable data systems for Stanford University's SLAC National Accelerator Laboratory:

"The low cost of computing power is going to be a central driver of what's possible in the next decade or so. It was not too long ago that computing power just couldn't achieve enterprise-wide sentience. Even if you had the right mind-set among data professionals, computing storage and cost were still prohibitive. That's continuing to change, and the key to progress will be this symbiotic relationship between capacity and skills: as we get 10-fold or 20-fold increases in capabilities, people will find new ways to use it. Then, of course, there are the ethical factors of programming algorithms that are becoming more and more advanced. Whether it's autonomous cars or sensors in critical infrastructure, algorithms are going to be in a position to make what could be life-or-death decisions. The people who train these algorithms will, themselves, need a lot more training and certification that takes into account the legal and ethical responsibilities that will increasingly go along with the business implications of their work. There may even be new organizational structures—like a committee approach or other governance—to undergird the integrity of those programming decisions."

A. Charles Thomas, executive vice president and chief data officer at Wells Fargo:

"Over time, you'll see more situations and contexts where access and curiosity around data are making a difference. I ultimately consider the chief data officer's charter to be anywhere we can inform business decisions at scale, and I think the future will show how that footprint expands into more and more lines of business. It's also going to be increasingly clear how this has to do not just with technology, but also with corporate culture. One important way to promote culture is to recruit talent who are data-literate from their previous training or work experience, and already 'get' the value of analytics. And I'm a very strong proponent of diversity, which I think we'll see more of in the coming years. The more you can get a variety of perspectives and backgrounds on your team, the better you can address the variety of technology challenges. This is the mind-set we'll need for tomorrow, an environment of analytic curiosity to help any given insight grow from interesting finding to a significant trend to that big cost-saving or profit-generating solution!"

A FINAL WORD

We sincerely hope you come away from this book as energized and inspired about the Sentient Enterprise as we first were on that auspicious day back in November 2013 when, together, your coauthors first seized on the concept and gave it a name. For all the reasons we've discussed, we believe the Sentient Enterprise is here to stay.

We're talking about more than just a business approach or an analytics strategy. We're talking about more than just technology. It's about capabilities, and where our efforts to mature those capabilities can ultimately lead. The Sentient Enterprise is our North Star that, with every success and every innovation, proves its relevance— indeed, its indispensability—as businesses sail faster and faster on an ocean of data into a future dominated and defined by that data.

Is it scary? Absolutely! Will it take time and investment? Without a doubt! But, as with any disruptive innovation, we must be realistic and optimistic at the same time. Success is possible if we embrace the changes and methods needed to fully leverage big data analytics for our businesses. Otherwise, we will simply be out of business, having lost out to competitors that did recognize this reality and are already building architectures and strategies to run with the opportunity and lead a revolution!

When and how we get on board this revolution makes all the difference. For the early adopters, it's about getting ahead of the competition; for the followers, it's about survival; for the unconcerned, it's about bankruptcy. Regardless, tomorrow is coming at us all like an unstoppable force, and we hope this book inspires you to start today.

Today! That is the operative word … our final word, in fact. What we're talking about can't be done all in one day, let alone one year. But we must embrace the mandate to build a more agile and Sentient Enterprise and take the steps to start building that enterprise. Start somewhere; start now; start today!

Acknowledgments

We owe gratitude to a great many people and industry partners who provided crucial assistance and insights in the writing of this book. We're especially thankful to Mary Gros, the mutual friend who first introduced the two of us on a hunch that our combined interests and passion for technology in the enterprise would lead to a lasting partnership (she was right)!

Thanks also to Chris Twogood, Sarah Howard and Katherine Knowles at Teradata for the many weeks of strategy sessions, interview logistics and other necessary tasks required to bring a project like this together. We're grateful to Shahed Ahmed and Richard Sheehe, with the Merritt Group, for their editorial assistance and interview support, and to our valued colleague Tom Davenport for contributing the foreword to this book. Thanks to Sheck Cho at Wiley for publishing logistics.

Finally, we must recognize the outstanding contributions of the data science leaders and their organizations who agreed to be interviewed for this book. Grace Hwang at Verizon; Brett Vermette at General Motors; Jennifer Felch at Dell; Kevin Bandy at Cisco; Gerhard Kress at Siemens; Jan Wassen and Bertil Angtorp at Volvo; Jacek Becla at Teradata and Stanford University; A. Charles Thomas at Wells Fargo; Bill Slough of the San Francisco Giants; Jay Nath of the City of San Francisco; Maksim Pecherskiy of the City of San Diego; and Partha Sen of Fuzzy Logix. Their willingness to discuss—in often candid and vivid terms—their own challenges and solutions has enabled all of us to learn and drive analytics closer to that point where a truly "Sentient" enterprise becomes a reality.

About the Authors

Oliver Ratzesberger is executive vice president and chief product officer of Teradata Corporation. Prior to Teradata, he spent seven years at eBay where he led their data warehouse and big data platform programs. He also has deep experience with open source startups. Ratzesberger joined Teradata in early 2013 as leader of the Teradata Research & Development software teams. As head of Teradata R&D, he now oversees a global organization including more than 1,900 technologists around the world.

Mohan Sawhney is the McCormick Foundation chair of technology, clinical professor of marketing, and the director, Center for Research in Technology & Innovation at the Kellogg School of Management at Northwestern University. Professor Sawhney is a globally recognized scholar, teacher, consultant and speaker in innovation, strategic marketing and new media. His research and teaching currently focuses on modern marketing, organic growth and business innovation. Prof. Sawhney advises and speaks to Global 2000 firms and governments worldwide and has written six management books as well as dozens of influential articles in leading academic journals and managerial publications.

Index